ROCK TAO
DAVID MELTZER

LITHIC PRESS
FRUITA, COLORADO

LITHIC PRESS

fine books for an old planet

www.lithicpress.com

CONTENTS

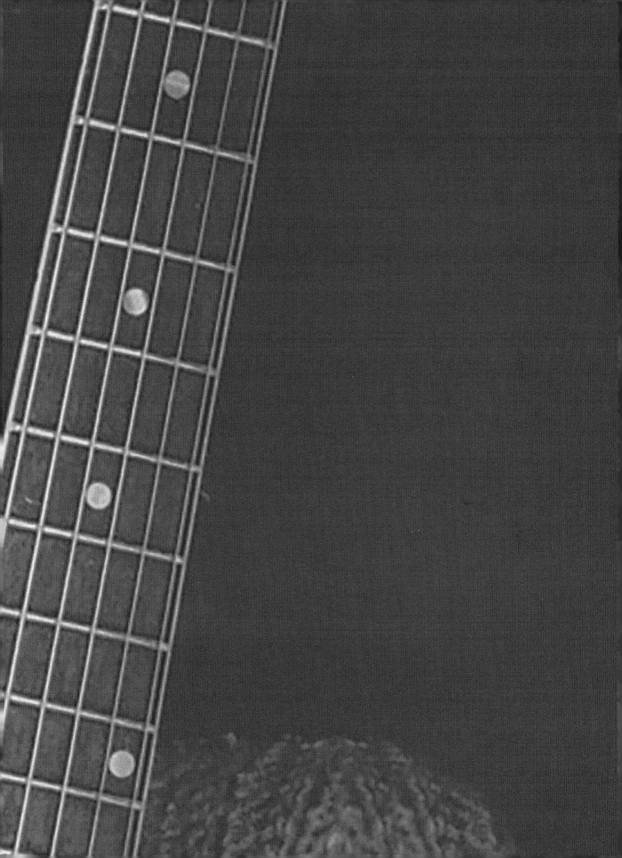

David was 28 in 1965 when writing *Rock Tao*. In a fact of fascinating coincidence, his peer Le Roi Jones/Amiri Baraka published the groundbreaking critical study of the Black American musical tradition *Blues People* in 1963 when he was 29. Although the works do not by any means align for an exact pairing, they do share some particular identifiable characteristics. Each was written by a poet at a relatively young age "admittedly and very openly shooting from the hip," as Baraka later put it[1]; working outside traditional parameters of "poetry" exploring their own self-identity through critical engagement with popular music phenomenon, by way of various apparatus, successfully offering up theretofore unexampled cultural critique. David's project does verge in a decidedly more experimental direction, while lacking the overt political/culturally-weighted nature of Baraka's endeavor—though *Rock Tao* is not by any means apolitical.

Rock Tao is in fact a rather erratic beast of a text encompassing a wide range of diverse material. Sparked from off David's listening to then local Bay Area radio station KEWB 91's broadcasts of the top rock n' roll songs of the day, between transcribing song lyrics (he couldn't just google them back then), David weaves the words of poets newsmen philosophers ad-men mystics and voices off the street together with his own running commentary creating a singularly awe-inspiring vast corpus. This makes the reading of *Rock Tao* both challenging yet also tremendously rewarding. David is ahead of the curve—his project stands up extremely well when compared with writings by the best cultural theorists out there (whose works in most cases hadn't even been written and/or had yet to published, particularly in the states).

This is true even as David is in large part figuring it out as he goes along. This being his first foray into a work of such length and scope, predating his many later ventures with anthologies interviews and essays—not to mention his teaching: his lecture notes regularly craft together a similar collage of source citations with his own critical commentary, and asides, as does *Rock Tao*[2]. He remarkably develops his own path in terms of form. The lessons he garnered in the formation of *Rock Tao* are most apparent in his handbook *Two-Way Mirror: a poetry notebook* written a decade later[3]. There is a similar collaging of textual

---

[1] Baraka, Amiri. "Blues People: Looking Both Ways" [new introduction] *Blues People: Negro Music in White America*. (New York: HarperCollins, 1999), vii.

[2] See Marina Lazzara's Afterword to *Rock Tao*, "Tonal Aura: David Meltzer and the Poetics of Collage". Lazzara provides a well-rounded perspective on the role collage plays in David's supernal abilities across-the-board as educator poet street theoretician.

[3] Meltzer, David. *Two-Way Mirror: A Poetry Notebook*. (San Francisco: City Lights, 2014). (Originally published by Oyez Press in 1977.)

citations and commentary organized into multiple numbered Parts.

The collaged form at work in *Rock Tao*, however, is of a far different nature, much less focused upon instructing the reader with a guided set of tips, and more akin to Walter Benjamin's *Arcades Project*, if anything[4]. While David's presentation of advertisements and news headlines serve as clear echoes of both the "Newsreel" and "Camera Eye" sections of John Dos Passos' epic Americana jaunt of a novel, *USA*. David continues Dos Passos' adventurous immersive exposé of America awash in media. The message(s) cut both ways. Viewer/consumer and marketer/propagandist alike drowning in the desire for further consumption. Also evident is the influence of Dada poet-artists collaging of found text and newspaper/magazine upon David's typing onto the page what the ear hears.

Kenneth Rexroth's introduction to David's *Tens: Selected poems, 1961-1971* makes note of how "For Meltzer the Word is Power, the power of the creative mystery."[5] Not so surprising then that in American rock n' roll lyrics David hears the Tao, or *a* Tao, ringing. David takes us on a deep dive, this is but one beginning of his lifelong pursuit to write The Book, slightly akin to Olson's "saturation job" in his remarks to Ed Dorn, i.e. that one project that gets you "in" forever[6]. Although if anybody was ever born "in" it was David, and he always kept on writing both before and after *Rock Tao* amassing as varied a collection of works (poems, essays, lecture notes, stories, translations, interviews, anthologies) as subjects covered (jazz, sex, nature, family, teaching, kabbalah, magic, art, the occult, popular culture, etc.).

Rexroth also describes David's own work as "a poetry of song, of the spoken word—'hear me talking to you,' as the title of a collection of autobiographies of leading jazz men once put it."[7] David is ever talking to himself as much, or even more, than to his reader. Never, however, in a solipsistic manner: David's inward gaze is always drawing from and robustly engaging with the outside world passing round. Also, as he instructs, "write what you want to read."[8]

---

[4] In 1965 little if any of Benjamin's colossal major work had yet been published. In fact, English translations of any of his work had just started to appear. *Das Passagen-Werk* [*The Arcades Project*] did not appear until 1982.

[5] Rexroth, Kenneth. Introduction. *Tens: selected poems, 1961-1971* by David Meltzer. (New York : McGraw-Hill, 1973), xiv.

[6] See: Olson, Charles. *A Bibliography on America, for Ed Dorn.* (San Francisco: Four Seasons Foundation: Distributed by City Lights Books, 1964).

[7] Rexroth, xiii.

[8] *Two-Way Mirror*, 72.

SERPENT POWER

FRI•SAT
DENO & CARLOS
728 Vallejo between Powell & Stockton
Minors Welcome

Massey

David's engagement with rock n roll culture went far beyond that of commentator/ appreciator. Having grown up immersed within the radio and stage entertainment world of New York City (where both his parents were professional musicians) before relocating to Los Angeles with his father, David played guitar throughout his life until his hands became too arthritic to manage the strings. For years, practically since his descent into North Beach from LA in 1957, he had been regularly making the coffee shop music scene in San Francisco. When not playing solo or filling in as needed backup, he played with his first wife Tina who sang, oftentimes singing himself as well. In fact, it was on those stages that he happened to accompany a young, new-to-the-city, fresh from Texas singer named Janis Joplin on more than one occasion. Shortly after completing *Rock Tao*, David embarked on a full immersion into its world when he and Tina formed the band The Serpent Power. Signed by the Vanguard label, although leaning more towards being noise-folk, The Serpent Power seemed on the cusp of breaking into the mainstream psychedelic scene of the time. Along with noteworthy mention in *Rolling Stone*, they played to a packed house at the Fillmore, yet the band (which included poet Clark Coolidge on drums) for various reasons called it quits. David and Tina continued as a duet but only released one album in 1969 (a second recorded album went unreleased until 1998). They continued playing and singing together, generally just at home for and with family and friends, until Tina's death from ovarian cancer in 1995.

A significant selection from the opening pages of *Rock Tao* appears in the David Meltzer/ Steve Dickison and Nicholas James Whittington co-edited issue of *Shuffleboil/Amerarcana 7* (Bird and Beckett Books 2017). David apparently made the selection similarly to how he often read from his work at poetry readings. Generally he'd have a stack of his poetry books next to him and apparently opening one book somewhat at random would start reading and then after a page or two he'd skip a few pages or put the book down and pick another up, again opening to a page somewhat at random and continue riffing his way along. Similarly, this selection from *Rock Tao* starts at the opening of Part 1 and occasionally skips over a passage or several passages, sometimes of up to half-a-page or more, much as if David was giving a reading from the galleys. The *Shuffleboil/Amerarcana 7* selection thus manages to get through roughly the first two-thirds of Part 1 in about half the number of pages. The passages David skipped over have here been restored.

It's important to state that *Rock Tao* is not a polished, 100% completed work by its author. The text provided here comes based off a photocopy of original galley proofs produced by Oyez press in 1965/66[9]. There are some corrections made in ink by David throughout the

---

[9] Oyez reluctantly had to drop the project and it was never picked up again.

galleys. While there are clear indications of breaks for each of the Six Parts given here, in the galleys the final section is labeled "Part 3 /The Rites". It appears highly likely that these galleys are actually two separate sets that have been wedded together. Starting with galley sheet 34 the text on the legal-sized galley page shifts from a landscape orientation of facing pages to a horizontal single-page layout with the text running the full-length of the paper. The galley sheet numbering also shifts at this point with the facing manuscript pages of galley sheet 33 numbered 53 and 54, respectively, at the bottom corner of each page while at the top of galley sheet 34 appears "Oyez—galley—20" and the latter numbering is thereafter consistently maintained. There is also an apparent short gap in the galleys as the focus of the discussion at hand transitions from Detroit/Chicago to Nashville/The South in Part 5.

Nearly all of David's original wording and spelling has been retained throughout except in cases of changes David made with selections as presented in the *Shuffleboil/Amerarcana* excerpt. The excerpt provided a kind of style-guide used for formatting the manuscript as a whole. This pertains to relatively small matters. For instance, in the published excerpt, the header "Current Myths" replaces that of "MYTHOS" in the galleys. This change, and a few others, made by David have been here retained and carried on with throughout the text for the sake of consistency. In addition, there have been a few silent editorial corrections of misspellings and some other slight adjustments in terms of tone and context.

Keeping editorial emendation to a minimum has meant leaving intact instances of undeniably offensive language, particularly regarding sexuality gender and race, which David would have revisited and altered. In later years, for instance, he moved away from universal use of the masculine pronoun, embracing non-gendered language. In 1965, however, David was still rather young, as has been noted. His writing throughout *Rock Tao* at times demonstrates the overwhelming influence of the wayward cultural drift of the times towards a white male binary manner of writing and way of thought. While there are hints of later discussions which he deeply engaged in regarding the complexities of the relationship between Black Music and its broad white cultural appropriation, David fails to satisfactorily deal with them here.[10] Yet readers should take heart in the enduring capacity his later work demonstrates for where he was heading even as *Rock Tao* offers but the briefest of glimpses. However retrogressive his views might appear, by no means did David continue to maintain them throughout the ensuing decades. Any glaring instances of white male heteronormative privilege only reflect the limited, blinkered stereotyping vastly prevalent in American cultural history. Thus providing needed reminder of not only just how far our society has moved along, but also how much further we all still need to grow

---

[10] For a much more sustained and informative engagement with these issues, see David's indispensable "Pre-ramble" to his anthology *Reading Jazz* (Mercury House, 1993) along with his "Pre-text" and "Sub-text" commentaries to his anthology *Writing Jazz* (Mercury House, 1999).

when it comes to possibly unhelpful tendencies toward hurtful categorizations too easily prevalent in our shared cultural lexicon.

While there's little doubt David would have made these further adjustments on his own, if given the chance, I am still confident that he would approve of the text overall as presented here. On a personal note, it's an immense pleasure to be taking part in ushering *Rock Tao* into publication after so many years. David was always very interested in seeing this happen. My deep thanks to his widow Julie Rogers for entrusting me with this project. I feel confident that David would be delighted with Lithic being the press to pick up this project from Oyez after so many years. He recalls his relationship with the Hawleys, the couple behind Oyez:

> Bob worked in the Rare Book/Western Americana room on the third floor of Oakland's long-gone Holmes Book Company. It was always a treat for me to go there and, in the late afternoon, drink shots of Jack Daniels, towered over by shelves of books [. . .] Bob was a great listener to early jazz, which was invariably on the record player. Dorothy was a gifted and creative bookbinder. They were both remarkably generous to us and I feel immensely grateful to them for that.[11]

I look forward to visiting Lithic Bookstore & Gallery out in Fruita one day and toasting David over whiskey with Danny and Kyle as the poems of tomorrow continue to arrive from out yesteryear.

Patrick James Dunagan
Nov.-Dec. 2020

---

[11] *Two-Way Mirror*, 9. It's also worth noting that Robert Hawley studied at Black Mountain College in North Carolina during the school's infamous final years when Olson taught and served as Rector. He came out west as did a number of other Black Mountain alumni. David later joined Black Mountain-affiliated poet Robert Duncan as core faculty of the New College of California Poetics program, which in many ways continued the pedagogical practices of Black Mountain.

BENEFIT SUN. DEC. 13 7:30-2

TO ORGANIZE A NURSERY SCHOOL

JAZZ JIM LOEW TRIO
ARNOLD ROSS TRIO
LOS FLAMENCOS DE LA BODEGA

FOLK HARRIET CARTER
BLUES JANIS JOPLIN
EDDIE MITCHELL
BALLADS DAVID AND TINA
COUNTRY DON GARRETT

A FILM BY BRAKHAGE

POETRY LEW WELCH
PHILIP WHALEN
RON LOEWIN SOHN

SATIRE HUGH ROMNEY
GARY GOODROW
JOHN BRENT
M.C.
PETER EDLER

COFFEE GALLERY
1363 GRANT AVE.

AND OTHERS

ADMISSION ONE DOLLAR
DONATION • NO MINORS

DRAWINGS BY
JENNIFER LOVE MELTZER AGE 3

Flyer for North Beach fundraiser circa 1963/64, just before David began writing Rock Tao. *Note Janis Joplin singing Blues, David & Tina [Meltzer] singing Ballads, poets Lew Welch and Philip Whalen reading Poetry. Drawing is by David & Tina's daughter "Jennifer Love Meltzer, age 3."*

ROCK TAO ROCKS ON

in its billboard cashbox heart, a record, the Product, is best
ONLY when it's duplicable & primarily REPLACEABLE
What is permanent, what becomes History, almost invariably requires Death
It is (I shd emphasize IS) a Business whose secondary product
is art, a popular (meaning saleable) commodity which pretends
to be Art but never is unless it turns platinum

ROCK TAO (1965)

I don't suppose I think much about the future;
I don't really give a damn. The only thing I'm afraid
of is growing old. I hate that. They get old and they've
missed it somehow.

— John Lennon

Tao has declined for a thousand years
Because the people valued their emotions.
When there was wine, they refused to drink,
And they set their hearts on fame in this world.
The reason our bodies are precious, is it not
Because we have but one life to live?
How much time is left in this one life?
It is like sudden lightning —
Like a boiling cauldron through a hundred years.
Regarding this self, what accomplishment is there?

T'ao Ch'en (Tao Yuan Ming)
c. 372-427 A.D.

But not in silence holy kept: the Harp
Had work and rested not, the solemn Pipe,
And Dulcimer, all Organs of sweet Stop,
All sounds on Fret by String or Golden Wire
Temper'd soft Tunings, intermixt with Voice
Choral or Unison; of incense Clouds
Fuming from Golden Censers hid the Mount.
Creation and the Six dayes acts they sung,
Great are thy works, JEHOVAH, infinite
Thy power; what thought can measure thee or tongue
Relate thee; greater now in thy return
Then from the Giant Angels; thee that day
Thy Thunders magnifi'd; but to create
Is greater than created to destroy.

From: *Paradise Lost* / John Milton

Introduction

THE IMAGE

Thunder comes resounding out of the earth:
The image of ENTHUSIASM.
Thus the ancient kings made music,
In order to honor merit,
And offered it with splendor
To the Supreme Deity,
Inviting their ancestors to be present.

When, at the beginning of summer, thunder — electrical energy comes rushing forth from the earth again, and the first thunderstorm refreshes nature, a prolonged state of tension is resolved. Joy and relief make themselves felt. So too, music has power to ease tension within the heart and to loosen the grip of obscure emotions. The enthusiasm of the heart expresses itself involuntarily in a burst of song, in dance and rhythmic movement of the body. From immemorial times the inspiring effect of the invisible sound that moves all hearts, and draws them together, has mystified mankind.

Rulers have made use of this natural taste for music; they elevated and regulated it. Music was looked upon as something serious and holy, designed to purify the feelings of men. It fell to music to glorify the virtues of heroes and thus to construct a bridge to the world of the unseen. In the temple men drew near to God with music and pantomimes (out of this later the theater developed.) Religious feeling for the Creator of the world was united with the most sacred of human feelings, that of reverence for the ancestors. The ancestors were invited to these divine services as guests of the Ruler of Heaven and as representatives of humanity in the higher regions. This uniting of the human past with the Divinity in solemn moments of religious inspiration established the bond between God and man. The ruler who revered the Divinity in revering his ancestors became thereby the Son of Heaven, in whom the heavenly and the earthly world met in mystical contact.

From: *The I Ching* / Trans. Wilhelm-Baynes

•

SONG OF THE POET (Tlingit)

It is only crying about myself
That comes to me in song.

●

All of us should know that art, science, and skill exist only to be conducive to joy, peace, unity, purity, respectability, to gratify our needs and help us serve our fellow men. This is also true of music. It is the remedy of all who suffer from melancholy and fantasy, disorders that ultimately make them desperate and solitary. But music has power to hold them in human company and preserve their minds; it drives out the spirit of witches, demons, and sorcerers.

Paracelsus

●

I kill a fly. Transistor radio blares in my head through a plastic earphone. *Love is an itching in my heart*, sings Diana Ross of The Supremes. Non-sacramental wine mixes with bread & cheese in my innards. The man who lives above me paces back and forth. I am clogged & I sit here before a writing-machine to tell you how God haunts these Godless times, but I do not pray, nor do I submit to ancient traditions, rituals, whose legacy of invisible & visible conclusions remain meaningful guides to me in my search for God. The search for God is the search for self, for the meanings within & beyond man. Rock & Roll, narcotics, comic books, pornography, movies, tv, are all ornamental to the quest.

To fill the void left by God's death we demand the quick abundant life & death of other gods & heroes. Constantly seeking new gods, new rituals, it seemed obvious to me that the Beatles were rightful heirs to shamanic traditions. Hermaphroditic gods to lead America's youth-cults into America's ultimate & massive marketplaces. The Orphic equations are unavoidable. Orpheus as John Lennon whose wife, Cynthia, becomes a symbolic Eurydice; Bob Dylan as Orpheus whose large fame can be likened to a race through Hades; Chuck Berry as Orpheus in the night-world of race warfare & sorrow. The Maenads, the Bacchae, are enacted by the predatory female followers, the fans, the fanatics.

●

Huge neon-ringed white whale worlds float not too high above our cities & do a superficial job concealing the dark & complex foundation of our nation. It seemed obvious when I began this work that our popular culture reveals more than it conceals about the condition of our souls, of my soul. I began examining what is famous in America as a way to sight those archetypal inventions peculiar to the land.

I became a motley scholar. My systems, charts, plans & schedules were as irregular as my knowledge. Any exciting sequence of information, a new word, a new name, would take me farther away from the map of my vision. Reading of angels & animas, mysteries & mandalas, numbers & names, made me realize that I could not be taught. I had to learn by examining myself, my origins, my own condition.

Some of my friends were skeptical.

—Popular culture's a monster. A monolithic hulking glut of trivia. Don't defile your Muse with loud music. Listen instead to the dreams of the dead. Grow an oriental beard to hide your sewn-up mouth.

•

One night a cherished moralist came to our flat to see our newborn daughter Amanda Rose & to celebrate Amanda Rose's mother.

When I told him that I was writing a book on popular music he said:

—What is it? Isn't it all sex & power? The men look like women & the women look like men or like little girls grimly frozen in eternal childhood. Those squealing teenage girls screaming at guitar-playing baboons just wanted to be fucked. What else? All that pent-up fire. The men grow farther from their source in women & are devoured by power-driven machinery seducing them into living with a false tribal dream of power thru the fertility of money. The women are left to contemplate the void. Terrible. What can either give to their children?

•

Many young look upon this time as one of profound betrayal. Betrayed by parents who themselves come from betrayal. Betrayed daily by a self-mutilating standard of ethics & morals, by a government whose reality seems that of betrayal; betrayed by a Judas economy; betrayed by safety-habits of thought-blocking public communications; it is no wonder that the young are easily guided into a Pinocchio carnival which prepares them for their entrance into the world of man.

•

From her dark Puritan garden of thorns, America has taken seeds to sprout a Garden of Eden peopled with a multitude of unsure Adams, perplexed Eves, phantom serpents, & wax apples.

•

America fights death by forming youth-cults who use concealment, flight, delusion, trick-mirrors, false faces, chemicals, glues, to halt natural age & wisdom. Even her leaders conform to the child-like ideal of father or the principal or the God with a 100 mile beard who checks off our good & bad deeds in a 100,000-mile-high Ledger.

Illusions of simplicity, illusions of complexity. Maya keeps our noses to the glass. Each mask becomes heavier & harder to remove.

•

Who fears new gods who are neither man nor woman nor child nor adult? how can these bards be the enemy?

This is not a moral history & could be, at times, immoral because it offers nothing more than observation.

•

Is there a way to penetrate that unknown core fixed in America's heart? If there is, it will be the same path leading to the unknown center of my own being.

This, then, is a poet's book, a book of myself, made with the self-invented tools of romantic scholarship.

•

ACKNOWLEDGMENTS: — KYA, KEWB, KDAI, KFRC, spoke & sung to me as I wrote this book. I used up 2 transistor radios, 29 9-volt Ray-O-Vac batteries & 4 earphones in the two year working.

•

I am grateful for the interest, concern, information, misinformation, good-will, friendship & criticism offered by: G. Legman, Peter LeBlanc, Guy Hesslegesser, Clark Coolidge, Ron Davis, Linda Hawkins, the S.F. Mime Troupe, Don Garrett, George Herms, Barry Olivier, Stevens Van Strum.

•

My deep thanks for the patience & faith given by Robert & Dorothy Hawley who gave me the box & let me open it.

•

San Francisco: 1964-66

PART 1: THE ORACLE, THE BODY

We got our own way of walkin'
Got our own way of talkin'
Gotta have fun anytime of the year don't cha hear
Gotta have fun spendin' cash
Talkin' trash
Girl, I'll show you a real good time
Common with me and leave your troubles behind
[…]
I don't care where you been
You ain't been nowhere
until you been
In with the In Crowd
             —The In Crowd: Dobie Gray

K!E!W!B!
TOTAL INFORMATION!
THE STANDARD OF AMERICAN
RADIO NEWS!
      booms forth.

The transistor god. His echo-chamber basso Yahweh profundo resonance surrounded by Morse Code teletype locust chatter.

—19 year old Gregg H Johnson, partner in the Woodside High School Marijuana Ring, was found hiding-out in the Hayward Hills with one-&-a-half pounds of Marijuana & a few ciggies which were immediately confiscated by arresting officer.

—*I'm just a soldier*
 A lonely soldier
 A long way from home
 Thru no wish of my own
        —Mr. Lonely: Bobby Vinton

—The Supreme Court ruled today that in order to be classified as a Conscientious Objector you must, first, believe in a Supreme Being.

TEENAGE PIMPLES & ACNE ARE NO PICNIC
NO STICKY OINTMENTS, GREASY CREAMS
A SPECIAL VITAMIN & MINERAL FORMULA

—The Animals stomped up a storm for 3,500 teenagers in the Cow Palace Friday night. The results: 4 teenagers stabbed, 1 kicked bloody, 1 policeman mauled. Riot squads from both San Francisco & Daly City took more than an hour to break up the crowd.

    There's something in the body that wants music to lead it into dance; music to give a moment its proper soundtrack; music to lead the imagination into new action, new dreams; music to be heroic within; mythic.

—When the show ended, thousands of screaming teenagers refused to leave. Gregory Price, 16, was jumped by 5 boys . . . kicks opened a dozen cuts on his face & scalp . . . Daryl Billups, 17, was slashed over the eye . . . gangs surged thru the throngs with knives and chains

MAKE IT TO THE FIRST WORLD'S FAIR FOR TEENAGERS, KARATE EXHIBITIONS, STOCK CAR RACES, DANCE & BAND CONTESTS, FASHION-A-GO-GO SHOWS, & MORE DURING EASTER WEEK VACATION AT THE SAN MATEO FAIRGROUNDS

—They jeered at police — sang under streetlights in a noisy frenzy . . . 3 youths emerged from the crowd clutching at deep stab wounds . . . all were taken to Mission Emergency Hospital . . . San Francisco sent its own animals to put an end to the show: German Shepherds from the Police Dog Control Unit

THE FLESH EATERS: BEYOND THIS MEMBRANE YOU WILL BE DRIVEN TO A POINT MIDWAY BETWEEN LIFE & DEATH!! THE ONLY PEOPLE WHO WILL NOT BE STERILIZED WITH FEAR ARE THOSE AMONG YOU WHO ARE ALREADY DEAD!!

He told me that he played with a rock'n'roll band at high school dances.
—I'm too young to play jazz-guitar for a living so we have this group & we've got a voice coach & a girl who choreographs us & we play for the kids. Y'know how it is, before a gig, I wash my hair two times so that it gets real fluffy & hangs over my face & every time I shake it the girls go crazy.

"In other songs the significant words are more elaborate. They are phrases fitted to the tunes, often by doing violence to the ordinary forms of words. The words are controlled by the tunes . . . Instead of 'I saw the great spirit travelling about,' we might have: 'I sawhawe the gre-heat sp'rit tra'ling 'bout, ham, ham.'"
—Boas: *Primitive Art*

—Ruby Small killed her husband, sawed off his legs to fit the corpse into the cedar trunk in their bedroom. Mother of three, she said she killed her husband because he made her dance in the nude and consume benzedrine tablets.
SPOT ANNOUNCEMENT:
— Hey, y'wanna avoid the Draft?
— Join the Army.

GO STEADY WITH A CLEAR SKIN! POLISH OFF BLEMISH. CLEAN OUT PORES. WITH BACTINE SKIN CREAM, YOU'RE IN!

—Mexican police arrested 17 year old Brian Krueger in connection with the slaying of 3 Mexican fishermen

The ordering a man goes thru. The ordering he constantly involves himself with in order to go on. He must constantly reconcile his need for gods & heroes.

Dear Brian (Jones): Last week I managed to scrape enough money to buy FIVE BY FIVE. I keep it by my bed so it's the first thing I see when I wake up. Why was I so stupid to persist in believing I shall meet you one day? I even pray about it and it's certainly not the sort of thing I should pray for when half the world is starving.

Love,

Margaret

bleat pulse spasm of Morse Code teletype: RKO Radio Tower volt bolts the Hot Wire

—Maxwell Taylor, Secretary of Defense, denied reports that the U.S. plans to send 50,000 more men to fight in Viet Nam . . . A Sunnyvale youth was killed in a head-on collision which was blamed on a locked accelerator . . . Frank Sinatra's daughter, Nancy, & her husband, singer Tommy Sands, announce their forthcoming divorce today in Hollywood.

—5 youths were with Caldwell in the car from which he fired two shots at a crowd of students in the Tik-Tok Drive-In near Balboa High School, killing Rodney & wounding John Santiago, 16

DON'T FORGET THE FAB BEATLES CONCERT!
TICKETS NOW ON SALE AT THE COW
PALACE BOX OFFICE!
MAIL ORDER ONLY.
TICKETS ARE $7, $6, & $4 PLUS A 50¢ HANDLING CHARGE
LIMIT OF 4 TICKETS PER CUSTOMER!

—The Rolling Stones are undoubtedly the most controversial... & the most unpopular with adults... here is the inside story as told to Ed Rudy by Mick Jagger, Brian Jones, Charlie Watts, Keith Richard, & Bill Wyman!! Only $2.98!! EXTRA: If you request it, each album will be autographed personally for you by Ed Rudy!!

Perhaps thru the loving of another, thru the worship of a hero, you can learn to love yourself; perhaps you can learn how to fully live within that portion of yourself you worship in others.

Trained to consume as soon as we're able. Trained to consume, to own; to have evidence, by-products, stuff. To own is to control. Goods give the dreams substance. To own the invisible is the first step towards vanishing.

DEFEND YOURSELF! WITH KETSUGO! (KETSUGO GIVES YOU ALL THE COMBINED ARTS OF SELF-DEFENSE FOUND IN JUDO, ATE.WAZA, AKIDO, YAWARA, SAVATE, KARATE & JIU JITSU)

—Who's your hero, your god, right now? I ask the young man leaning against his immaculate new Chevrolet Nova drinking Grape Cola out of a can, a cigarette in his other hand.

Brightly shined high-heeled, high-ankled Beatle-style boots. Long hair slapped back, straight & greased. Black tight pants. He was Chinese (the wisdom of centuries) & he had a transistor radio plugged in one ear. Never looking straight at me, never keeping me out of sight, he replied: — What are you talkin' about, man?

"Go ahead. Keep on sinning — rock and roll, smoke, drink, swear, play with sex, act big and brave, act like you don't need Jesus, act like everything is going to be all right. But don't you ever forget that one day soon you will have to look into the face of Jesus! One day your fun will turn into terror!"

from: *Chicken* by Dave Wilkerson. Gospel Publishing House, Springfield, Mo.

"The trouble is that the people here expect show business folk to act big, talk big, dress slap-bang in fashion — and wear stacks of greasepaint. But I'm glad to say we still don't want to conform. Even if we get ourselves hated."

—Brian Jones (a Rolling Stone, rhythm guitar)

SPOT ANNOUNCEMENT:
—Join the modern U.S. AIR FORCE & be among the hippest!

Flamenco dancer boots, shoulder-length hair, tight black pants, thready tweedy sports jacket & faded black t-shirt. His face a strange machine of fast talk & twitching smiles.
—Man, I took some meth before coming here. Yesterday. Still going (smile). Man, you should really listen to Manfred Mann. Too much (smile). Wow, those Chuck Berry copycats really bug me. But the Stones, man, nutty. The way Keith takes off & digs in (smile). Too much (smile). Keith nearly kills himself killing me (strange laugh). Man. Banging his juice-axe into a live mike. I tell you, man, you gotta be nuts to be a rock'n'roller. Out a sight. They're all out, mad, man. All juice-axe players are just mad, man, insane (smile) & way way out of it.
—What's the name of your group? I ask him.
—The Victims.

Wherever you see yourself, you see something of the hero, something of yourself made final.
To own time, consume timelessness.

—16,000 American troops are being sent to the Dominican Republic . . . Those on the ground watched in horror as his chute failed to open & he rocketed to earth at the sky-diving exhibition given in Glendale early this afternoon.

I, with my gods, cannot dismiss the quality of another's gods. My cycles have been made meaningful by revelations brought to me by gods of music.

The time of Shoshtakovitch, Sibelius & Stan Kenton; my ring finger turning black with the Lone Ranger atom-ring on it.

Going to a Jazz at the Philharmonic concert (we were 15 years old) with my beer-drinking buddy Henry after hitting his parents' liquor-locker (they were in Florida on vacation) screaming GO GO GO GO GO! when Buddy Rich & Gene Krupa had a Norman Granz drum-battle on stage & when Illinois Jacquet started honking one note on his saxophone while the J.A.T.P. All-Stars jammed behind him. During Billie Holiday's set Norman Granz took the microphone from her & told us all to shut up & listen to Lady Day & stop stomping on the floor & for God's sake stop throwing paper cups off the balcony. Listen—

"All that which occupies the natural self of man must either be made to disappear or must be transformed in such a way as to render it transparent for the inner spiritual reality, whose contours will then become perceptible thru the customary shell of natural things.
        from: *Major Trends in Jewish Mysticism* by Scholem

—Use the think-tank as much as you use the gas-tank. That way, says Ron Dunne, KEWB dj, you'll live a lot longer.

All myth begins as news.

My childhood mystery glyph was the Pet Milk can: cow within can within cow within can.

"What little blues I heard in England ain't nothin to talk about. Can't tell the men from the women."
        —Jimmy Reed/*Hit Parader*: Jan 1966

—My girlfriend gets horny watchin' us rehearse (smile) so I have to make her leave, y'know. We're all, see, plugged into our amps, right? We're workin' on a groovy Stones song, right? The rhythm guitar says, Man, I'm not loud enough, I can't hear myself. Okay (smile) so he turns his volume up but I'm lead guitar, I can't hear my break, right? so I turn my volume up . . . then the Fender bass can't hear himself because we're so loud so he turns his dial up & the drummer's hittin it as hard as he can & wow in just a few seconds we're full blast (smile), right? right in it, the zone, man, inside of sound, right inside of it! Wow.

> PASTOR HITS ROCK 'N' ROLL "FRENZY"
> Atlantic City (N.J.) — (AP) — A California pastor called rock 'n' roll music a "modern noise" which, he said, drives teen-agers in to an emotional frenzy, produces hypnotic trances and contributes to juvenile delinquency and crime.
>   John Loos of Riverside, Calif., pastor of a Seventh Day Adven-

tist Church, urged churchmen, youth leaders, parents and teachers and leaders in the entertainment business curtail music which "incites youth into activities in which they would not normally engage"

—I don't have to BELIEVE in god! I KNOW god!
— Rev. Robert Alexander, Director, Temple of Man

The self in the limit. To find the limit is what self is.

"I remember Cocteau playing drums in a jazz band as if it were a very difficult mathematical problem."
—Ezra Pound/*Paris Review*: Summer-Fall, 1962

Ecstasy is central to all religion. Worship is habit after the fact of ecstasy. There must be an experience, or the promise of Experience.

What is fame today, or any day, does not have to mean that what is famous has a quality to it, has the quality that endures beyond a moment. To be famous is to be on time, in your time: to be in correct sequence.

Judgement? What is judgement?

Do I say this is good because it pleases me?

Yes, that's what I do. This is judgment.

THE BEATLES' KISSING CONTEST!

On the coupon on these pages, you'll see a blank area. What we'd like you to do is make a kiss-print in the space. Here's how you do it. First, put your lipstick on carefully. Then practice making a kiss-print by blotting your lipstick on a tissue . . . put your lipstick on again and blot on the coupon.

The girl whose kiss-print most closely resembles the kiss-print of the Beatles' dream girl (and we're not snitching on what she's like) will be the winner.

Just one more secret — the prize in this contest will be received by the winner the next time the boys are in the States. If you want to practice puckerin', go ahead. This prize just might be a smacking good one (if you know what we mean!).

After the hero creates himself, the rest is gravy.

—Plane crash: 37 killed . . . Congressman calls *The Spider* the filthiest, foulest, dirtiest magazine published on a state-supported campus . . . London newspapers, this weekend, filled with critical editorials directed at LBJ, as they call it, his Big Stick policy of intervention in Viet Nam & in the Dominican Republic.

I sit here, Saturday night, plugged-in. The transistor radio earplug in my right ear. A transfusion of secrets. The radio in Orpheus's Rolls Royce. Words are to be translated from the songs, the news, the commercials. Musics in my head. They rattle & crash & soar, the news goes on & on, — a fusillade of commercials.

To be plugged-in is to be able to be & not to be. Like wearing shades. It's a way of being inside-out.

—*I told you once and I told you twice*
But you never listen to my advice
You don't try very hard to please me
With what you know, it could be easy
Well this could be the last time
May be the last time, I don't know
Oh no, oh no
        — *The Last Time*: The Rolling Stones

—This FRIDAY, Bobby Mitchell and Tom Donahue present at the Civic Auditorium, the Rolling Stones, in concert — and that's not all! With them will be
    Hey, Mr. Tambourine Man, play your song for me . . .
the nation's hottest new group, The Byrds, along with The Vejtables, The Ratz, Paul Revere & The Raiders, The Notables, and many many more great groups to entertain you!

Weather: No tidal waves as forecast this afternoon.

Song is the bridge transporting the dreamer into his particular dream, carries the mind over the void with little or no vertigo.

The dream's speed lingers after the song is over. The bridge dissolves like a haiku.
—I don't have any of my records at home, Adam Faith says to dj Perry Roberts.
—What about having a legacy for your grandchildren?
—I wouldn't want to inflict them with it.

The fool is the best dancer. He doesn't know he's a fool. The saint is a statue.

—*I know a place*
Where the music is fine
And the lights are low.
I know a place
where we can go.
    #9/*I Know a Place*: Petula Clark

—When they decided they were right, the record company put an estimated million dollars into promoting The Beatles, says Faith.
—They could've failed anyway, says Roberts.

—But they didn't.

The son of a Chicago minister, the 32-year-old singer was riding the crest of a wave of national popularity when he was shot to death in a Los Angeles motel . . . To RCA Victor, Sam Cooke was big business. To songwriters he was an annuity and a hit maker. His income exceeded a quarter of a million dollars a year and before his death, he felt that he had just hit his groove.

HEAR WIDESPREAD SECRET CONVERSATIONS THRU SOLID WALLS! 500-SHOT AUTOMATIC SLINGSHOT DEVICE PICKS UP 2-WAY CONVERSATIONS WITHOUT CONNECTING TO PHONE!

GOLDEN OLDIE:

—I got stung by a sweet honey bee
  Oh, what a feelin' came over me.
  It started in my eyes,crept up to m'head
  Flew to m'heart till I was stung dead.
  I'm done, uh-huh, I got stung!
  Mmmmmm, yeah, Mmm-mmm, yeah!
          —I Got Stung: Elvis Presley

Revolt seeks order through disordering. Elvis was a revolution. The Beatles, a revolution. All revolutions are revelations that speak meaningfully to the young. I never thought of it that way becomes: That's the only way to think about it & you are that much older.
    Success seeks order.
    Lennon & McCartney earned 4 million dollars in royalties on their songs last year.

"Out of about two-thirds of a million people in both cities, over a quarter of a million died as an immediate or later result of the bombings:

	Daytime Population	Deaths
Hiroshima, 1945	400,000	200,000
Nagasaki, 1945	270,000	122,000

The injured will continue to suffer and die into the indefinite future."
          From: FACT SHEET ON THE EFFECTS OF THE ATOM
              BOMBS AT HIROSHIMA AND NAGASAKI

—No one will understand
  What I've gotta do
  I've got to find a place to hide

With my baby by my side
She's been hurt so much
They treat her mean and cruel
They try to keep us far apart
There's only one thing left we can do
We gotta keep searchin', searchin'
Find a place to hide
If we gotta keep on the run
We'll follow the sun
　　　　　　—#22/*Keep Searchin'*: Del Shannon

—It's the Garbage Men NOW at the Zanzibar Club

"Don't tell me where I been until I been there. It isn't there if I ain't there!"

No one wants to be free. One wants moments of freedom. One wants to be freed of oneself. For moments. One wants memory restored, yet one would forget. No one is free who wants it.

—*Every evenin' when all my day's work is thru*
I call my baby and ask her what should we do
I mention movies but she don't seem to dig that
And then she asks me why I don't come to her flat
And have some supper and let the evenin' pass by
By diggin' records beside a groovy hi-fi
And I say yeh, yeh
Thar's what I say, yeh yeh
　　　　　　—#15 / *YEH YEH*: Georgia Fame

　　Repeating helps define. It is ritual. Ritual becomes habit. Habit is order.
　　Take the seed to your nest & eat it slowly; grow a tree in a place where trees grow high to shut out the sun whose light the seed needed.

　　　　　ROCK'N'ROLL RIOT
　　　　　Kagoshima, Japan—UP—A policeman died of a heart attack and
　　　　　13 people were injured Monday night when 12,000 teen-agers
　　　　　mobbed the box office trying to get seats for a show by Japanese
　　　　　rock'n'roll idol Teruhiko Saigo.

—*She comes around here*
Just about midnight

She makes me feel so good
I wanna say she makes me feel allright
　　　　#5 / Gloria: Them

The LIFE reporter asked me questions for an article he was writing relating the Berkeley student revolt, student revolt in general, with the Beat Generation of 10 years ago. (At moments I felt like one of the old-timey relics of the back pages: 103 year old last surviving member of the Donner Party or Gomorrah, interviewed on how it is to be alive in these newfangled times. You don't tell 'em how your body's killing you & how day to day you hold on, held together by the pain that reminds you that you're alive. You gotta tell 'em, the whelp, about General X's weird sex habits & how many cups of whiskey you drink each month to remain alive. They come with questions that they have already answered & are, instantly, disappointed if you cannot answer the answers they are prepared for you to answer. After all, you're not the only 103 year old last-surviving member of Armageddon.)

—Do you think that the student revolt of today is like the Beat Generation of 10 years ago? (The tiny Sony transistor tape-recorder spinning its spools to capture my dull answers.)

—No. The Beat movement was a passive thing: a retreat, a public & private surrendering. The kids revolting today are, actually or figuratively, fighting for what they believe they want, protesting against what they believe is no longer useful or right. Revolt is healthy; it is outward, it is growth. The Beat movement (which I always thought preceded the Beat Generation by 10 years) was apolitical, except for Ginsberg or Corso — but they were leaders & a movement is the followers of a revolution.

—You know, the reporter says, — I was a member of what they called the Silent Generation. That was a proper name, I'll tell you. None of us (he is 32; went to Rutgers) could act, could enact revolt, tho many of us wished to.

"The people we're killing in Viet Nam are the same people whom we've been killing for years in Mississippi," SNCC's Bob Moses, speaking at a service for Schwerner, Chaney and Goodman, observed that the bodies had been found on the day newspapers reported the American bombing of North Viet Nam. He said that what we must learn from all these deaths is to stop killing.

—Wow! here it comes!
　Here comes the night!
　Here comes the night.
　Oh-h-h, yeah.
　　　　#28/Here Comes the Night: Them

Who are heroes? what is fame?

—Do you realize, I say to Bob, Americans are demented with time & fame; we're dizzy with it. Your time to be young is so fast that you age before you begin & spend the rest of the time looking back for something lost

How long do you have to be young, devout & loving to the gods of youth?
Your time to be young is so fast that you age before you can begin.
What is famous?
What you want to buy is what is famous. What you want to consume, what you want to own.
What devours you that you in turn, would devour.

FILMCLIP (color): Beatles concert. Harrison & McCartney sing jaw to jaw before a round microphone. Lennon to his own mike & behind the three, Ringo bashes away at the drum kit, elevated so he can be seen clearly. George & Paul sing *She Loves You*
        She loves you, yeh, yeh, yeh
        She loves you, yeh yeh yeh yeh
shake their fabled hair, yodel a nerve-braiding bay & the audience goes wild
        Well I saw her yester-day-yi-yay
Paul & George smile the knowing smile of gods singing for the devout yet know a secret beyond themselves, their song, their screaming fainting fans
        Yeah yeah yeah yeah
& while they sing, they talk of other matters with their eyes

Worship is a revolt. New gods to create men in their own image.

HOWARD'S
THE MODZIP
Tall dark & handsome
boot maintains an
exciting pace with
quick-action side-zipper
and high heels. 10" tall,
made in England.

GOLDEN OLDIE:
—*He sort of smiled and kissed me goodbye*
But the tears were beginning to show.
As he drove away on that rainy night l begged him to go slow,
But wether he heard I'll never know.
        (—WATCH OUT WATCH OUT WATCH OUT: screech & skid then crash &
        explosion of impact — Molly's closet; Pandora's box; opened; deluge)

I felt so helpless,
What could I do
Remembering all the things we'd been thru'.
In school, they all stop and stare.
I can't hide the tears
But I don't care.
I'll never forget him
Leader of the Pack
>   (—sound of a 200 cc Harley gunning in an echo-chamber)
>   *Leader of the Pack*: The Shangri-Las

Absolute speed. Car, motorcycle, jet, rocket. Surfboarding, skydiving, sidewalk boarding. Move. Challenge & control speed & motion; in constant momentary harmony with destiny.

Speed changes the landscape. When you go fast enough, you see only speed. See the shape of speed on unlit roads at night in hills rising above electric cities. It's only what's before you, what headlights illuminate:

(in Dean's fireman red Porsche Speedster, going up the Hollywood hills faster & faster, cornering curved roads leading around black shadowy forms; shooting down the Pacific Coast Highway faster & faster, full moon in splinters on the Pacific Ocean: luna confetti — snarling angry engine bouncing off hills — going through farmlands, top down, smell of sour soil, top down, smell of wheat & tilled earth damp with night dew.)

To be going nowhere; to abolish space with speed. Speed-angel carries you out of yourself & into the service of Speed Heaven, cluttered with heroes. They are all young. Only the young can match escape with speed. When you get older, speed become suicide.

When you're speeding, speed is everything. There's nothing more. What abstractions come to mind are quick, instinctual: fast doom flashes, hitting a wall so fast you're ejected from the smashed car — propelled without pain into the sky.

—Members have been observed wearing various types of Luftwaffe insignias and reproductions of German iron crosses. They have been observed wearing metal belts of a length of polished motorcycle drive-chains which can be unhooked and used as a flexible bludgeon . . . In addition to the patches on the back of Hell's Angel jackets, the "One Percenters" wear a patch reading "1%-er". Another badge worn by some members bears the number "13." It is reported to represent that 13th letter of the alphabet, "M" which in turn stands for Marijuana and indicates the wearer thereof as a user of the drug.

from: The Attorney General of California's report on motorcycle groups

It becomes a flight from burning cities.

There's no turning back unless you would turn to salt or break your neck in a head-on collision

—Don't want nobody that don't want me
 I ain't gonna love nobody that don't love me
 I don't need anybody that don't want me
 I ain't gonna have nobody that don't love me
          #30/*Too Many Fish in the Sea*: The Marvelettes

Is fame speed?

I tell my wife that we are famous to each other & our children are famous to us as we are famous to them. Isn't that enough? But even in the family, a structure, a hierarchy (division of angels).

Order is based on comprehension of it.

PEOPLE

ALLEN GINSBERG, American poet who caused a controversy a few years ago with his "Howl" was expelled from Czechoslovakia. (He had gone there to reign as king of a May Day youth festival) and his diary of his activities confiscated.
THE BEATLES, the British rock 'n' roll quartet, will be listed in a new edition of *Who's Who in America*, it was announced by publishers of the reference book in Chicago.
YEVTUSHENKO, given permission to leave the Soviet Union for the first time since he was publicly censured by the Russian Government two years ago, travelled to Italy on a reading tour.
S.F. Chronicle / May 23 / 1965

Is what is famous that which we worship? — an idea we wish to serve & ascend to?
What do we worship: God, gods or heroes? What is the difference, what makes for the sameness?
What is an artist?
Why do I question; why do you question?
To order, to clarify. To maintain intelligence, to be able to live with people independent of worship. To challenge; to submit.

"It is more barbarous to eat a man alive than to eat him dead."
          — Montaigne

Is fame an assumption in accord with an assumption already made? Is it faith or lack of it?

The hero is speed. Pursuit.
The hero moves. Speed
  Campbell in the Bluebird on the salt flat straightway; James Dean in the Spyder, Super (faster than a speeding bullet) Man. Speed reorders the body hit by Gs, force of gravity pulls flesh off face revealing the skull.

—When you speak of music, do you rank literature under music or not?
—I do, answers Plato in *The Republic*

  The mirror anticipates death. Our form, our face, attacked by time.

  What is young is speed & to worship youth is to worship youth's speeding to death. Only the old worship youth.

FULL-SIZE
Compact
ELECTRIC
GUITAR
with amplifier
ONLY $19.95

THE BEATLES
Watch them grow their own hair
Live in your own room!
Yes, can you imagine, you can even give them haircuts! You can actually have the fabulous Beatles growing in your own room!

  Suddenly you see your face, your form, what it will be & you see it in the mirror, or in a store window, stopping there to pat down your ample hair

THIN LEGS
Try this new
amazing
scientific method
DINGY TEETH MADE RADIANT WHITE

FAT LEGS
Try this new, amazing
scientific
home method

PLAY GUITAR IN 7 DAYS
or money back

Your face is your mother your face is your father your face upon those faces & all of those faces do not look as you would look.

It is looking not to see, it is the face within that looks for itself.

HOW TO BE LOVED and be LOVED!
only $1.00 plus these 2 valuable fact-packed books FREE of extra charge
1. *Art of Kissing* . . . explains, discusses 25 kinds of kisses
2. *Modern Love Letters* . . . 47 effective model letters for any situation

GLAMOUR WIGS IN A CHOICE OF BEAUTIFUL COLORS and STYLES

Lovely NAILS in a FLASH . . . with NU—NAILS, artificial fingernails

The roots of the music, its earth, is black, it is the Negro's music first of all & finally.

It is unfair to compare Howlin' Wolf singing his *Little Red Rooster* with the Rolling Stones' version of it.

Nothing is the same. Hence, tradition. Art begins as imitation.

—To feel you all around me
And to take your hand
Along the sand
Ahh, but I may as well try and catch the wind
[. . .]
When rain has hung the leaves with tears
I want you near
To kill my fears
To help me leave all my blues behind.
                    #13 / *Catch the Wind*: Donovan

A Marinda girl was dragged 200 feet by a speeding vehicle while her parents stood by in horror screaming to the motorist to stop but he couldn't hear them . . . she suffered multiple fractures & is not expected to live.

Clarify, order: your universe, the world, your robes, your trance, & your dance.
What about money?

"A beginning songwriter would get the same money as we get — a penny for every record sold . . . The main thing is to get a publisher . . . get a record." (Jeff)

"You also get money in addition to sales every time a song is on the air. BMI keeps a cross-country file. If you start getting a lot of air play, TV shots, million-sellers, then you need a lawyer and an accountant. You'll know when that time comes." (Ellie)
 —Jeff Barry & Ellie Greenwich, songwriters: *Hit Parader*/May 1965

Q. Do you feel your popularity is based on your sound or on your image?
A. Both.

"One of the tragedies of the whole civil rights movement is the inability of the white person to distinguish significant Negro leadership. For example, any Negro who achieves a certain amount of prominence — a Cassius Clay or Willie Mays — when he utters something about race relations is treated as an expert."
 —Whitney Young / President of the Urban League

You feel your hero's face is your face when you move in a certain way, enact a brief drama as if him. To feel his face as your face, a mask, an actual weight. A transformation that, moments later, is revealed when your eyes spy the stranger in your mirror.
 Bobby Vee celebrated his new 5 year a contract with Liberty by purchasing oriental art objects for his Hollywood house.

It's all wrong. Dancing to black music played by white teenagers with long hair & soft faces. We dance alone. White man's black man impersonation: a masquerade wiggling, jiggle, waggle of a rubber-dance;
 in neat Italian suits, bright porcelain shoes. The women in their costumes dance on crowded floors alone. Men & women apart from each other dance before each other absorbed within themselves, sealed by the loud electric music;
 final racial arrogance: a self-fuck pantomime.

Current Myths:
John Lennon, the one wearing spectacles offstage, is going blind.
Paul McCartney has a serious illness and does not have long to live — rumors similar to ones circulating in America about both Rick Nelson and Elvis Presley.

The Tao of it. Jungle-black, mountain shadow, the other side of the moon; lair of womb —black the signifying color of the female principle. Capricorn-black, grief-black; Black Country: Northern Egypt: home of the Black Arts; Black Bull of Egypt; the Black Friars; black animal of sacrifice; black opal; the Devil in the blackbird; black death; animal of sacrifice; Prince of Darkness

The Tao of it.

A wild snowstorm in the mind; white sheet covering a sudden corpse; white paper to begin marking up with black signs; daylight living edging quickly into well-lit locked homes as night darkens the lines, blurs the simple; living, except in dreams, with light fighting terrors of darkness; the endless dark of the looked-into well (your breath an echo repeating down its stone ribs); submit to the electronic butter/fudge of TV, following light like moths to the bulb, the flame. What greater sorrow to see men & women righteously destroy their lives, the lives of their children, the course of the race, defending & upholding without yield Black & White (— *It can only be one or the other: it's either Black or White*) — No turning back but the burning of their skin in fire of ultimate atomics — the light to lead them into blackness; & white the color of purity virtue goodness the robes worn by vestal virgins, the raiment worn by the resurrected Christ; white is the tabula rasa; it is the seed of man.

He can only see himself. Eyes shut, walk into the world wearing self as an emblem for magical protection.

"26. It should be understood that war is the common condition, that strife is justice, and that all things come to pass through the compulsion of strife."
"115. People do not understand how that which is invariance with itself agrees with itself. There is a harmony in bending back, as in the case of the bow and the lyre."
    — Heraclitus

—*When I'm watching my TV*
 And a man comes on and tells me
 How white my shirts should be
 But he can't be a man
 'Cause he don't smoke the same cigarettes as me
 I can't get no satisfaction
 No, no, no Hey, hey, hey
 That's what I say
        #8/*I Can't Get No Satisfaction*: The Rolling Stones

Time is memory of it. Music is time: a theme fragment, a few sung words, & one remembers a specific moment gone. Time is the evidence of loss. Song reduces the collective dream to the most recognizable substance. What is complex in a time, the form of a time's dream, is partially known in songs. Time is the realization of destruction: it is also the awareness of creation's process.
    The heart needs regular demolition.
    We submit to the heroic because the heroic is what we possibly are. The song challenges nothing. It fills in gaps. It's a tool for the creation of memory.

"However, the basic experience is ecstatic, and the principal means of obtaining it is, as in

other regions, magico-religious music. Intoxication also produces contact with spirits, but in a passive and crude way . . . the use of drums and other instruments of magical music is not confined to séances. Many shamans also drum and sing for their own pleasure; yet the implications of these actions remain the same: that is, ascending to the sky or descending to the underworld to visit the dead."
— Mircea Eliade: *Shamanism: Techniques of Ecstasy*

—I can heal the sick and raise the dead
I can make you little girls talk right out of your head
I'm the one, yes, I'm the one, I'm the one
I'm the one, the one they call the seventh son
#19/The Seventh Son: Johnny Rivers

All the abortions, creams, pimple pills, pastes and powders, cigarettes; candies: the white black nutty creamy gooey messy sick sweet chlorinated artificial fecal anxiety narcotics; all racial misinformation, self-protecting mental deterioration, all of it essential to the human heart, money to the manna-fixer, work for lithographers, announcers, electricians, accountants, Japanese transistor & motor bike manufacturers (—we never warred with any continent nation or ideology that did not, finally, beat us with our own dream); all the records, magazines, shoes, stockings, Q-tips, dogfood, all the STUFF is HABIT'S food. Who's not an addict? nor hooked to an idea, a way of life, a shifty ideal? Man's the habit-mammal whose survival & fulfillment depend on ritual & habit. Before one can open the soul to power, the energy that defines it, one must practice obedience.

Addiction is order. It gives purpose to the disorder of life. Millions of middle-class Americans are addicted to pep-pills, sleeping pills, tranquilizers, legally obtained thru physicians who do not have the time nor bent to be shamans or magicians.

The imagination's aliments destroy the body that houses it.

—A strong force drove me to the graveyard
I stood in the path; I saw the shadowed grave
And then I looked and saw my sweater
Lying there upon her grave.
Strange things happen in this world
#36/Laurie (Strange Things Happen): Dicky Lee

My daughter Jenny is 4 years old & she's crazy about Ringo Starr. My wife Tina is 29 years old & last night dreamt she went out on a date with Ringo. Howard is 25 years old & has a snapshot of Ringo entering or exiting an airplane looking, as Howard puts it: — Out of his gourd, man.

Current Myths:

Jacob says Cain heard from Esau that Joseph turned the Beatles onto pot when they were in New York. Ringo asked John if it was all right. John said he'd ask their manager. Their manager said why not. Bobby Dylan was there. They all got high together. All except John.

—One day I was hailing a cab on a street that was filled with puddles from a recent rain. As the taxi stopped for me, a teenage boy ran over and threw his jacket over a puddle. I was completely stunned and then embarrassed for both of us.

I stammered, "Please, please, pick up your coat. you shouldn't do that for me. you shouldn't do that for anyone."

— Barbra Streisand

JFK's murder began his true leadership. We worship lost youth more than ancient wisdom & thrive on both public & private sacrifices. Kennedy is worshipped for what he might have been. The unknown is the basis of religion. Speculation is the dream pivot. Anybody might possibly be he-who-was-not or he-who-might-have-been.

PROTRY is today's expression — a mirror of our times. It keeps pace with tomorrow's rocket to Mars, yet it safeguards our heritage.

Watch for John Snyder, the voice of the Neo-Generation, and his dynamic social critique *World a Go Go* — it dares to say what you are thinking . . . Available soon.

—I've had a fever ever since this morning, Jean Cocteau said.
—And I should say that Edith Piaf's death has made it hard for me to breathe.

—Cocteau died two hours later.

You make a rose afraid to grow
You make the wind forget to blow
You make the sun up in the sky forget to shine
And you're drivin' me outta my mind, now
        #14/ *Voodoo Woman*: Bobby Goldsboro

"I believe in a paradoxical form of life. I don't believe anything is wholly right, both right and wrong. There is a thin line between. There is a Chinese proverb that 'Life is a search for truth and there is no truth.' It is important to know that truth carried too far becomes destructive."
        Norton Simon / Businessman: *Time Magazine*: June 4, 1965

Components: Alternatives
Collective worship destroys the man it worships. Worship degrades. It makes the singular plural. It diminishes a man into a fragment.

Worship is a bondage the hero willingly submits to.

Heroes who submit to worship are failures.
We also worship failure.

"I LOVE RINGO!"
Teen Dream Scarf
Your choice of a lovely, high-quality head scarf. 2 feet square, made of heavy hand-rolled blended silk. PERMANENTLY HANDPAINTED with the name of . . .
>*YOUR FAVORITE SINGER
>*YOUR FAVORITE MOVIE STAR
>*YOUR FAVORITE TV STAR
>*YOUR OWN BOYFRIEND
>. . . or even
YOUR OWN NAME! Mailed GIFT-WRAPPED in a clear plastic envelope.

Youth's smooth face assumes the face of the Invincible One. His body swaddled in the moment's correct drapery, he assumes he is what fame instructs him to be; walks down Market Street, a strange dance, masculine fantasia: spread leg cowboy hero, motorcycle speed king, killer commandos talk, brute stomp, heavy-foot clomp, champ dance, a stiff stride not belonging to the legs attempting it. Heroic snapshot. Catches the sight of his body in windows: bulging, bending, on a car fender; his face in the enemy's eyes before him; his face in Her eyes passing him by; he is passed & he passes.

—*It's not unusual to be loved by anyone*
It's not unusual to have fun with anyone
But when I see you hangin around with anyone
It's not unusual to see me cry
I wanna die.
>#30 / *It's Not Unusual*: Tom Jones

Snorts. Lights a cigarette. Sucks death in. Gushes the smoke out, lets the stuff stream out of his nostrils; — cascades over his mouth which bites at it, sucks it in again, puffs out a new snake & tries to form a smoke-ring; looking at me, yet not looking, he looks away & wants to be seen as much as he also wants to be invisible. So he can watch himself being seen &, if possible, see what you see & be sure that what you see is the hero he is miming.

—The first three months under contract were pretty hectic . . . (you're sent) out on a round of parties . . . every night . . . parties . . . and before long you notice all the faces you see at all the parties are the same. Three months of that and I was sick of the whole thing. It's not bad now, though.
>Karen Jensen / Starlet

A leader is always standing before you with an army standing behind him.
The hero stands alone. That is why he leads the young.

—Bullfighting fascinated him (James Dean) for a while and he practiced cape movements at home to the accompaniment of appropriate Spanish music.

FRUG THAT FAT AWAY — DEATH OF THE DIET

"Our government right now is slowly being undermined by the Communists. No one hears about it because bigshots make sure it doesn't leak out. Crying in their soup, not hardly. "If Bob Dylan or Joan Baez or P. F. Sloan or Phil Ochs don't bring these things out to the younger generation, who will?"
from a letter: *Hit Parader* / April 1966

Today is a time of all time & of no time. I speed thru it holding a thread of history. Or I sit in the middle of it & it sounds like the earth turning. All that preceded me is before me. Evidence everywhere. We assemble our histories continuously.

Centuries of Eastern & Western art & wisdom available in all forms — books, photos, records, tools, weapons. Time & technics translate the evidence left by all civilizations. We can return to a place that is perfect & complete centuries after its ruin.

What is famous?

Anonymous painters, bards & craftsmen once served God & directed their best to the best they believed possible within man & beyond him. The anonymous marks on time. It is more than nostalgia that leads us to, or back to, great works.

LA SHEER
Bares your shoulders — see the barely safe effect! This sensational Cotton wonder has that true Frederick's fit that snuggles your curves . . . Keeps you trim . . . made entirely of RUBBER, works like a portable steam bath. While you wear it, pounds melt away . . . holds you with fantastic control. Invisible under a dress or leotard

I attempt to re-discover. To seek & to see the order of things. To look & re-see what has been seen often enough yet never recognized by my eyes, my heart. To find my face, my form, to bridge the dark & face the light, take my chances & continue the learning.

—*Throw away the lights, the definitions,*
   And say of what you see in the dark
   That it is this or that it is that,
   But do not use the rotted names
      from *The Man with the Blue Guitar*: Wallace Stevens

"The secrecy surrounding the boys' wearing of the *upi*, a tall, awkward and probably uncomfortable hat made of palm leaves, which conceals the hair. The *upi* is put on while the boy's hair is short, and he wears it until initiation, never taking it off in the presence of women until it is ceremonially removed. On its removal, the women suddenly discover the mysterious secret of men: they have long hair. The main purpose of the ceremony is to surprise the women with the length of the hair."

from *Symbolic Wounds*: Bruno Bettelheim

A hero lives his life in the memory of his heroic act. A single heroic act can alter a man's life. If he survives he will speak of it until he dies, collecting souvenirs & documents to wallpaper his archives.

If by accident a man is made a hero, he will attempt to create a myth from that error.

(—Do you remember X who used to be in the movies? You must remember him, well anyway, I know X. He's a personal friend.)

By contact with a hero, a man can have a meaningful secondary fame.

```
*  *  *  *  *  *  *  *  *  *  *  *  *  *  *  *  *  **
*  AMERICAN OPINION BOOKSHOP  *
*   BOOKS  *  *  BIBLES  *  *  FLAGS    *
*  *  *  *  *  *  *  *  *  *  *  *  *  *  *  *  *  **
```

Thru all of this, an instinct to aid the intelligence to survive even its own heroes.

—He didn't fly down from heaven with white wings on his back
He blew in from Kansas City in a big red Cadillac
Yeah, he said he made his bread playin' rock 'n' roll
I ain't no angel, angel
But I don't want anybody but you
[. . .]
You know he sleeps 'til sundown and he keeps me up all night
And when it comes to lovin'
That boy is out-a-sight
Yeah, you know he makes me lose my self-control
He ain't no angel
But that's alright.
　　　　#19 / *He Ain't No Angel*: The Ad-Libs

Many of the great gods of American letters were also gods who failed: Jack London (suicide), Vachel Lindsay (swallowed a bottle of Lysol), F. Scott Fitzgerald (an alcoholic), Hemingway (shotgun), Hart Crane (jumped into the sea), Bodenheim (shot to death in a Skid Row flat);

(Lew Welch once said:

—Say, Dave, did I ever tell you my definition of fame? It's when people know you that you don't know.)

"All of us failed to match our dream of perfection."
    William Faulkner

The impossible hero (Superman, Capt. Marvel, Batman) accomplishes impossible feats & enters the realm of god-symbols that inspire an early sense of man's tragic bent towards failure.

My childhood comrade & enemy was Jordan Cohen who worshipped Superman & Al Jolson (as played by Larry Parks). Jordan lived in the corner apartment with his mother, a loud, husbandless, nervous shrew-bitch whose shrieks kept the block awake at displaced intervals day & night.

l knew Jordan wasn't Superman (having pounded his head on cement when we fought) but Jordan had deep doubts. He wore glasses & Clark Kent wore glasses.

I first saw him reading the latest Superman comic book, crossing Linden Blvd, a two-lane boulevard in Brooklyn. He was crossing against the light. Cars zipping by slammed on brakes, horns honked, but Jordan paid them no mind (up!up! & awaa-yyy) & continued at his own pace to cross the thoroughfare, turning to the next page.

—Hey Y'DUMB JERK! dumb-ass! 4-eyed schmuck! whaddaya doin! ! asshole! ! ! screamed a shocked-white motorist whose car stalled.

His day of wingéd disgrace: poised, like Esther Williams, Jordan stood on the lip of the apartment roof in a home-made Superman suit: a pillowcase cape with S written on it in lipstick, jockey-shorts & an undershirt with S in lipstick in its center.

—UP! UP! & AW—

—JORDAN! JORDAN COHEN! You dumb bastard! What in God's name'r' you doing up there!! his mother hollered at him.

—Aw, ma, for God's sake, lemme be, I'm Superman.

People gathered below to watch.

—Y'get the hell off a that roof or I'll kill you, you jerk, you dumb bastard! stupid, stupid! she screamed, veins in her neck pulsing against flesh, her distended in anguish, terror & rage (her sometime lover out the back-way; his afternoon ruined).

—Oh God, Jordan, please, PLEASE, get down, she moaned, — y'stupid stupid dumb jerk bastard.

& Jordan perched there like a ballet dancer, wind furling his pillowcase cape, turned around & left the roof, walked downstairs. His mother beat him senseless.

—Yeah?

—Yeah!!

& we'd pick at each other's nerves. I'd grab his dirty shirt & try murdering him again.

His lips were wet; his glasses glared; his curly hair was heavy with dirt & grease; he smelled of rancid butter, unwashed underwear.

Later on, we'd play Al Jolson.

—Awww, MAA-mmy! he'd sing on bent knee — I'd walk a mill-yun miles for one a your smiyuls, mah ma-ha-ha-mee

   & we'd laugh.

A BIZARRE TWIN PEAKS "TORCH"

David Schmuck 19, proclaimed himself a Buddhist monk last night, doused himself with gasoline and lit a match.

Doctors at Mission Emergency Hospital said 95% of his body was covered by third-degree burns. They do not expect the boy to survive.

FRED: Honestly, John, are you happier now than in the early days in the little clubs in Liverpool?

JOHN: I'm probably happier. In those days we had peace and quiet but we were broke — and I wasn't married. There are lots of things that aren't so good and lots that are better. It all balances out. Being rich is no worry for me. I don't believe it ever is — that's just what the rich people say. I like being rich and I think other people do, too. My son will be second generation rich which is a problem I haven't worked out yet — where to send him to school and so on, you know.

A few years later, reading National Geographics instead of comic books, Jordan began knocking over baby buggies. After I had moved away, I heard that he'd been committed to an institution for trying to rape a girl much younger than he. Jordan was, at that time, 15.

"You smell of gasoline," she told him.

"I've been helping Jim work on his car," he replied.

That's Odd, Miss Schmuck thought, because Jim (a family friend) doesn't have a car.

SCRIBBLED

He left the house again, returning after a few moments and asked for pencil and paper. He scribbled quietly at the kitchen table, the sister said, and then read aloud what he had written.

"Buddhist Monk. Inquire at 4l0-A Fairoaks. I die for all mysterious things."

"What does that mean?" Miss Schmuck asked. But David only smiled enigmatically and went out the door.

From source to source. The round dance done.

—40 yr old mother of 3 held off police until they tossed teargas bombs thru the window where she surrendered & they discovered the body of her husband shot thru the heart. She has been placed in a psychiatric ward for observation.

—5 shots from a speeding auto

—Minotaur seizes maiden & escapes police-barrier due to distraction caused by a 4-alarm fire two blocks away

—Star fullback, halfback & quarterback for the Hollywood Bisons confesses morphine addiction at closed-meeting of the Big Brother Club local chapter of which he has been a member for over 4 years

—Of 1500 dead only 150 were estimated to be the enemy in recent battle-campaign in Viet Nam

—Tomorrow's announcers are out there in the audience today. They're working in Greyhounds in offices and they're frustrated they want to get into broadcasting they really do they want to do something with their lives. Call collect to XYZ School of Radio Broadcasting and you too can be a dj.

— Authorities seized the white man responsible for the shooting of the Negro Army captain in Bogalusa

—Headless, clutching at his vanished parts, Orpheus crashed thru the picture window & fell bleeding from numerous wounds upon the rug overturning a tv tray & the half-eaten dinner upon it.

Part 2

—Woo, it's growing
Every day it grows
A little more than it was the day before
My love for you just grows and grows
Oh Oh Oh Oh how it grows and grows
And where it's gonna stop
I'm sure nobody knows
>>> #24 / *It's Growing*: The Temptations

Whatever it is, it is not what it seems to be.
Change is a burning. A triumph above flame like the Phoenix reborn.

Fire[1]: the burning Buddhist monks of Vietnam; Giacometti, the sculptor — "But the thing, the suicide, that really fascinates me, is burning oneself alive. That would be something." Fire renews what it destroys. The burning man alive with fire (David Schmuck) races over a hill to escape his pain & embrace his spirit. D. H. Lawrence, the emblem of the fever of his tuberculosis. Fire turns the meat of flesh to fragile ash, lightening the ponderous massiveness of the body into particles taken up by the wind, or slowly eaten by the earth.

Fire suicides are becoming more frequent in America. Yesterday a Marine immolated himself because he was deeply unhappy about Marine doctrine & training. A few months ago an elderly lady in Detroit ignited herself because she was outraged by the American war effort in Vietnam.

Speech as fire; art as fire. Flame's heat as a cleansing power. Fire as a baptismal rite.
The pyromaniac; the ecstatic.
Puberty is a blaze of birth. The body is ablaze with growing. The spirit is flaming & its fire illuminates the edges of night. The inner-heat creates a raw-nerved screaming torment boiling the heart. The loins plunge into lake water to cool. A plume of steam shoots from the phallus into the water that holds it up in watery gravity.

---

[1] Fire, the 3rd element. Triangle, pyramid, obelisk: point up to symbolic fire. Basis of worship's primal source. (Tableaux: lightning strikes dry hunk of wood. Ignites it. The caveman, symbol of unconscious origin, bends to the wonder & terror of flame.) God speaks to man with thunder & lightening. The sun's little brother. Agni. Ptath. Vulcan. Bast, the cat-headed goddess; Sekmet; the lion goddess. Sacred fire of the Greeks guarded by the Vestal Virgins. Gabriel. Prince of fire. Fire of martyrdom, saintly fervor. St. Anthony Abbot; St. Agnes. Fire of sex, the flame of life. Fire-sticks. Mastery of fire is one of the shamanic goals: swallowing live coals, walking on fire (cf. *Shamanism* by M Eliade. NY, 1964; *Myths, Dreams & Mysteries* by Eliade. NY, 1960). Gtum-mo, Tibetan psychic heat: a naked monk sits in lotus-pose on the ice of a Tibetan mountainside, melting the area wherein he sits. Kundalini, the inner energy & fire of spirit described in Yogic writings, which when released uncoils shoots up thru the chakras of the spine, central nervous system's web, the rings of being, to burst thru the head's dome as a flaming lotus. Sakti.

Ye wavering forms draw near again as ever
when ye long since moved past my clouded eyes.
To hold you fast, shall this time endeavour?
Does my heart still that strange illusion prize?
                    from *Faust*: Goethe (trans. G. M. Priest)

A man inside the youth's body stretches within the boy's form.

Alchemic & chemic fluids erupt & combust inside the tortured body. Skin explodes into pimples, welts, blackheads, acne, whiteheads. Hair grows on flesh once smooth; a pubic jungle on the crotch. Behind & before him is the female. Before heroic acts & after them awaits a female — moving ahead, turning the corner, pulling her shadow behind like the train of an evening gown.

Body and spirit seek fulfillment with the creative principle. Necessary polarity; essential duality. (No new vision, yet clearing of sight reveals the depth of the old vision.) Puberty is also the bringing forth of first vision central to his life's duration, acknowledged or not.

Body bulges, drains, becomes lean, gets fat where fat is foolish.

& all the mirrors, magic or real, cannot aid nor distract time's work.

•

walks down the street
Quick. His mind's a movie. The street is set for his walk. Women flock to the famous.

—*Baby I'm yours*
And I'll be yours until the stars fall from the sky
Yours until the rivers all run dry
In other words: until I die.
Baby I'm yours and I'll be yours until the sun no longer shines
Yours until the poets run out of rhymes,
In other words: until the end of time.
            #25 / *Baby I'm Yours*: Barbara Lewis

You can't honestly indict a 2-year-old for imitating a 4-year-old's obnoxious traits & you cannot condemn a child for misinterpreting the adult fantasy. Youth is in physical & emotional upheaval & there is revolution within & around youth. In the chaos & terror of it he must make his first attempts to reach out, with shaken faith, towards that which represents some kind of order.

—*DO all a-them things now*
Get yourself a girl now
Get down on the floor now

Dance like you never danced
Get down on your knees now
Say, do the sweet pea now
Step to the left now
Step to the right now
Do the boomerang and, girl,
Do all a-them things now.
         #29 / *Do The Boomerang*: Jr. Walker & the All Stars

   This is a time when a person could say that what is immoral is now moral. What order? Whose laws?

. . . said Richard Burton when he heard of his ex-wife's marriage to 24 year old Jordan Christopher, singer & leader for the rock 'n' roll group called the Wild Ones: *"Oh, my God!"*
Said Jordan Christopher about his new wife who is 12 years his senior: "As far as I am concerned, it was love at first sight."
Said Jordan's father, a Macedonian bartender in Akron, Ohio: "I don't see what she can possibly see in him."

"Christian people will vanish. Teen-agers will be running through the halls in schools looking for their Christian friends but they will be gone. The radio and TV sets will be buzzing about the mysterious disappearance of people from every nation."
         from *Chicken*: Dave Wilkerson

"Natural man is not a 'self'— he is the mass and particle in the mass, collective to such a degree that he is not even sure of his own ego. That is why since time immemorial he has needed the transformation mysteries to turn him into something, and to rescue him from the animal collective psyche, which is nothing but hodgepodge."
         from *Psychology & Alchemy*: C. G. Jung

   Hierophany of periodicals, of cigarette butt particles (girls grabbing them off the stage after a Rolling Stone concert), of jellybeans (thrown in votive tribute "hurt you," said Ringo Starr) (full-page photo in LIFE of a teenage girl on her knees looking upward, face contorted in an ecstasy of pain & devotion, holding a jellybean stepped on by a Beatle); particled bedsheets off beds Beatles slept on auctioned off 10 highest bidders (lavender sheets Kim Novak slept on cut into ties & sold at high prices) — not absurd. Abides with the sexual spiritual indirectness of these times. Deliberate misdirection: a magician's device to distract.

   A pessimistic radio-engineer I know came up with the following plan:
Instead of mustard-seed amulets why not spermatozoa of movie stars — or smears of

menstrual blood from movie queens — sealed in glass, worn around the neck or, why not, minute extracts of turds dropped by great stars. — We'd call the amulets: Uncommon Scents or . . .

—*When I grow up to be a man*
  Will I dig the same things that turn me on as a kid?
  Will I look back and say that I wish I hadn't done what I did?
  Will I joke around and still dig those sounds
  When I grow up to be a man?
  Will I look for the same things in a woman
  That I did in a girl?
  Will I settle down fast or will I first wanna travel the world?
  Now I'm young and free, but how will it be
  When I grow up to be a man?
  Will my kids be proud or think their old man is really a square?
  When they're out having fun
  Yeah, will I still wanna have my share?
  Will I love my wife for the rest of my life
  When I grow up to be a man?
            When I Grow Up To Be A Man: The Beach Boys

Fame is childhood. An overwhelming reduction of the tangle into a simply sighted X.

Fame is an ideal innocence; an order of reality for the many who would without it, live in formlessness.

O'Hare Inn, a luxury motel, announced it is banning rock 'n' roll musicians as residents . . . The action was decided after the Byrds, a longhaired singing unit, tried to enter the dining room in bare feet during their recent stay at the Inn and were turned away

"Our youth now love luxury. They have bad manners, contempt for authority; they show disrespect for their elders, and love chatter in place of exercise. They no longer rise when others enter the room. They contradict their parents, chatter before company, gobble their food, and tyrannize their teachers . . ."

            Socrates: quoted in *Dear Abby's* (Abigail Van Buren) column

Nearly 50% of the United States is under 25 years of age.
25% of the population are teenagers.
Economists regard the teenager as a new income class to contend with;
Some teenagers receive a weekly allowance that would equal what a destitute family of 6 would receive from Welfare.

Allowances are based on parental income. One can assume how parents compete, between themselves, in affording their children the highest allowance on the block — and how their children's allowance would become a status-symbol for the parents as well as the children.

"The record business is a worldwide enterprise with sales in the U.S. alone reaching some $600 million to $700 million last year and growing at a rate of 10 per cent a year. It is also a business that depends more and more on the teens and the sub-teens, who dig $250 million out of their piggybanks and their allowances every year for records. Altogether they buy 40 per cent of all albums sold and a staggering 80 per cent of all singles."
Newsweek: October 11, 1965

"The current estimate is $13,000,000,000 a year in freely disposable cash — cash not required for the teenager's own maintenance . . . and those statisticians who count the youth market — the age range of thirteen to twenty-two rather than fifteen to nineteen — say that is has already reached about $25,000,000,000. . . teen-agers now are estimated to own nine percent of all new cars and an uncounted number of used ones. . . (teen-agers) accounts for more than half ot the attendance at all motion pictures, buys much more than forty percent of all records and cameras and more than one-fourth of all cosmetics."
from "In The Time It Takes You To Read These Lines The American Teen-ager Will Have Spent $2,378.22": Grace and Fred M. Hechinger / *Esquire*, July 1965

". . .rising allowances and swelling incomes from part-time and summer jobs this year will put a whopping $12 billion into the jean pockets of the nation's high-school boys and girls. This about equals the total output of South Africa and adds up to an income of $670 per teen year."
Newsweek: March 2-1, 1966

To consume is to also be consumed. (Again, fire.)
Great Pharaohs gathered their loot together to die with it. The gold, the fine cloths, the carvings, trinkets, cutlery, etc., held sacred powers & were essential for the journey toward Isis.
But the children with their abundance of stuff & goods glide into unreal adulthood. The consuming mania is a reflection of the adult world they live within. Seeking understanding, a connection with their elders, the adolescent attempts to emulate them. But what doctrine their peers offer do not fill the void. Suddenly the youth is a young adult, married, no plans for children, living in a recent low-budget tract home, new car bought on time as well as the essential TV & other home appliances. They both work. Meet in the morning, meet again at night. The purpose of their cooperative venture is vaguely satisfied on weekends when they can go shopping for new objects for their home (whose ceiling is beginning to welt &

termites can be heard at night boring thru the cheap wood beams). The river runs into the sea & the sea stretches out as far as the eye can see.

"The money economy freed the individual from the dominance of the patriarchal authority, and enabled him to seek self-actualization through personal relationships of his own choosing. Man became increasingly at liberty to develop his own ethical ideals, and to live the good life as he saw fit. Freedom from ancestral tradition also facilitated the rise of higher religious ideals which insisted on loyalty to the universal brotherhood of man, rather than to the immediate kinship group. The growth of the market had a twofold effect: it destroyed man's feelings of emotional, economic, and spiritual security; but at the same time it established him as a rational person capable of free choice. It is the great task of the twentieth century to frame institutions which will restore man's feeling of rootedness without sacrificing the integrity of the individual."
　　　from *Magic, Myth & Money*: William Desmond

　　　The Marketplace, an invention guarded by doppelgangers, is an alchemical event engaged in the maintenance of the consumer carnival — a carnival not unlike the one Pinocchio was led into to be transformed into an ass.
　　　The Marketplace is in constant quest for total domination, transforming its dependents into a collective ideal to clothe, shoe, feed, emotionally pacify. A way, a method, to program the mind until the mind becomes a repeating servant to consuming. A Way is always sought by advertisement hive-dynasties to make Gold come out of the common ore; to make the common ore transform itself into gold before a post-hypnotic consumer eye.

—*Sunshine, lollipops and rainbows,*
　Everything that's wonderful
　Is what I feel when we're together.
　Brighter: than a lucky penny,
　When you're near, the wrinkles disappear, dear,
　And I feel so fine
　Just to know that you are mine.
　　　#22 /Sunshine, Lollipops & Rainbows: Lesley Gore

　　　Trained to be consumers before we were born by parents who are consumers. Our very birthings are now, as a rule, performed automat-style on Hospital assembly-lines that do everything but package & label the newborn infant. Birth has been reduced to the production of consumer goods. (Abortion is still illegal perhaps because a potential consumer is destroyed.) Babies being born & unborn in that frenetic silent-movie speed of today's young. What is moral? Whose ethic forbids abortion? What law is the true law?

JOKE: Christ returns to 20th Century earth & cannot understand the high prices on merchandise he sees displayed on a city street & chides various store-keepers for their profit-hungry greed.

He spots a carpenter repairing a cross on the steeple of a church & climbs the ladder to the top to talk shop.

— What are your wages, sir? he asks of the carpenter.

— $5.73 an hour with time & a half for overtime.

— Why that's outrageous! says Christ. The carpenter returns to hammering the cross securely to the steeple.

— Why the work you're doing is truly worth half that wage! Christ continues to berate the carpenter until the carpenter grabs ahold of Christ & begins nailing him to the Cross, muttering as he hammers:

— You'll never learn will you?

—A 19 yr old deaf-mute oblivious to the frantic warnings of a fast-approaching train was run down & killed.

—2 Marin City boys, ages 8 & 9, were cited by Sheriff's deputies for deliberately burning 2500 copies of the SF Examiner Sunday insert sections . . . 3 tons of comic & feature sections were burned in a garage.

—A 16 yr old West Berlin boy blew his brains out because he had to have his Beatle-length hair cut off.

(Suicide, matricide, patricide: the gossip of the press is rich with it. The adolescent act of identity. The boy who shot his father because he wouldn't eat fried chicken the boy brought home for their dinner. The girl who knifed her mother & step-father to death in their bed during an act of love because of the noise they were making. Not wanting to go to school because he was tormented by his comrades, a boy begged his mother to let him stay home. She refused & he went upstairs to cut his throat. Murder & suicide are also our youth's rites of liberation, a wedding with destiny. From passive suffering & loss, the youth breaks from his night to act. To be seen, known, to be freed from origins which refuse him.

The family becomes fragmentary, divorce a commonplace, & children born in such circumstances instinctively try to find their mother, their father, seeking their blessing.

So many of these murders are in self-defense which the Law cannot comprehend.)

—*Well let me tell you 'bout the way she looked,*
The way she acted, the color of her hair.
Her voice was soft and cool,
Her eyes were clear and bright,
But she's not there.
  She's Not There: The Zombies

America lives in cities or in suburbs of cities or in tract communities (which are neither city nor suburb) which spring up in order to justify freeways. (Tract-housing grows faster than trees, creates jobs. & is a more practical form of freeway landscaping.) 53% of the nation's population is concentrated in 213 urbanized areas that together occupy only 7% of the nation's land, according to the U.S. Bureau of Census.

"How people feel about giant agglomerations is best indicated by their head-long effort to escape them. The bigger the city, the higher the cost of space; yet, the more the level of living rises, the more the people are willing to pay for low-density living. Nevertheless, as urbanized areas expand and collide, it seems probable that life in low-density surroundings will become too dear for the great majority."
    from "The Urbanization of the Human Population": Kingsley Davis / *Scientific American* Sept/65

"What is a city? It is a community of substantial size and population density that shelters a variety of nonagricultural specialist, including a literate elite."
    from "The Origin and Evolution of Cities": Gideon Sjoberg / *Ibid.*

The gasses of industrial growth conceal the sun. Waste from factories pollutes the waters factories piss in. Population grows like cancer. Educational systems are not working on a new generation with questions & contempt for the examples offered to emulate. Men are going to doctors with pains that are, upon examination, pains of the spirit & not the flesh & women are at odds to liberate themselves from biologic & emotional lineage. The children continue to storm the cell's gates to break thru, attack another cell, break thru, until the struggle tires them out & they are trampled on by children breaking thru their cells & the disease-metaphor continues to break thru: a factual (& metaphysical) plundering evident anywhere you look.

GOLDEN OLDIE:
—*When good friends prove untrue*
And all the things they do to you,
They make you feel so bad,
They make you feel that you haven't a reason for livin'
So when you feel you could throw in the towel
And just give in,
Darlin, reach out for me.
Don't worry. I'll see you through.
        Reach Out For Me: Dionne Warwick

Without memory of lack, how can one live with abundance?

A demonology could be compiled out of the monstrosities of Suburban life. The infernal Tract(atus) that binds the middle class to a realized ghetto. In 5 years, a tract community looks 20 years old & 10 years behind the time. (Soon, I believe we might see ghost tract-home towns.) Measured landscape, uniform dwellings, lack of space of privacy. Mythologemes made out of the constant attempts of tract-dwellers to assert their assaulted individuality: the man who planted trees & bushes on his front lawn immediately after the landlord's Demolition Patrol tore up the last group he'd planted; or the tale of that gentleman farmer who let the grass grow ankle-high on his "landscaped" front grass-plot to protest his sudden realization of outrage & entrapment). A phenomenon researched and developed in America for Americans. The children born are born in the hospital adjunct to the community & raised in an abundance of cars, clothes, tv — the whole community linked to gargantuan marketplaces called Shopping Centers (the *raison d'être* for a compleat tract commune).

—Now ... LET THE EVERLY BROTHERS TEACH YOU GUITAR! World famous singers will teach you their Lightning quick way to play Rock 'n Roll, Country, Western, Gospel and Popular songs in one week. PLAY THE EVERLY WAY!

(SHOPPING CENTERS I HAVE SEEN; —an inside aside.
My cherry taken by the less-than-monumental Pay-Less Shopping Center in Mountain View, California. Unless one craved for more curious & out-of-the-way goods & stuffs, one could find almost everything one would ever want (lawn-mowers, food, food, food, radios, tvs, books, records, frying pans, vaginal jellies, toilet plungers, 6ft tall Panda Bear Toy, 25lb War Games Kit; staples, needles, pins — my mind bogged down by it — popcorn stand, hotdog, hamburger, juice stands, a continental restaurant, cotton candy, donut counter — machines, vending machines — one showed a plastic toy car put together before your very eyes: put 50c in the slot & the machine behind glass obeys by stamping, cutting, twisting the wheels onto, a toc plastic toy car & then deposits it out of a chute, still hot, into your hand — the food food food in depth: the bread counter had more brands of bread than I believed possible & all of the meats bright red & sealed in Saran Wrap in green cardboard trays & all of the produce bright green, yellow & red neatly packed in their green trays, covered with Saran Wrap which creates a brilliant patina on the food there were two (not one) Speed-Check Stands (for 5 items or less) &, at least, 25 regular check-out stands that were all, I said all, in operation — the cash-registers very discreetly concealed to look like adding machines; the change & cash drawer is not attached to it but placed under the counter — the beautiful bland music of Musak pervades the market-mumble of babbling consumers, in their trance — one could buy all of his clothes & shoes there — you can cash your checks there; get money-orders there — they give away merchandise-redemption stamps — I went in there unwilling to be impressed & left it, glazed, a frustrated consumer overpowered by the objects of my affection — you could spend at least an hour at the soup-can section ...)

Engine, engine #9
—Comin down the railroad line
* I know she got on in Baltimore.*
* A hundred and ten miles*
* Ain't much distance,*
* But it sure do make a difference.*
* I don't think she loves me anymore.*
        #16 / *Engine Engine #9*: Roger Miller

The tract/center environs produce an amazing statistic of juvenile criminals. A new child prodigy monster criminal at his formal press conference says, "I raped her first & then all of us raped her & then we decided that we couldn't rape her anymore because she really was too out-of-it to make it worthwhile. We took turns dismembering her without hunting knives & put parts of her in the trunks of our cars. I couldn't help laughing when I heard her head bonking in the trunk, hitting the spare tire."

Crime, an immoral conclusion, has always been presented as a high form of heroism & idealism to the young & old alike in the outlets of popular culture

If the ideal is the lack of one then why condemn the imagination of our child-prodigy murderers?

What do kids have who have everything their Parents never had? Like the young Buddha, tract-children are offered a life without balance or reason.

The car as surrogate mother/Temple-whore.

The oldest of the bandits was 16. They all came from upper middle-class homes & their specialty was demolishing sports cars: dismantling them & dumping the parts into SF Bay. It took them no longer than 15 minutes to accomplish the vandalism. They drove their own sports cars to the appointed scene of the crime.

"I do not address myself to nations but only to those few people among whom it is taken for granted that our civilization does not fall from heaven but it, in the end, produced by individuals. If the great cause fails, it is because the individuals fail, because I fail. So I must first put myself right. And as authority has lost its spell, I need for this purpose knowledge and experience of the most intimate and intrinsic foundations of my subjective being, so as to build may base upon the eternal factors of the soul."
                    C. G. Jung

GLENDALE Current Myths:
A teenage hot-rod club met after school at a drive-in & were usually harassed by a pair of Policemen whose coffee-break coincided with the club members' coke break. Insulting remarks were indirectly made about long hair, tight pants, & the shiftlessness of youth today.

One afternoon the kids waited for the Policemen to enter the drive-in & then, while one of the kids spotted thru the door, stripped the patrol car of all its moveable parts. One art the kids understood was The Car. Crawling inside & outside of the Patrol Car, the group of young craftsmen had it stripped in under 10 minutes eye time. After their coffee was done, the two Policemen returned to find their car parked on blocks.   Over a 6 month period, every part was returned in paper bags to the doorstep of the Police Station.

All revolutions create law.

Police Lt. O'Neal's 19 year old daughter was raped by a gang of "filthy bearded hoodlums" & 3 days later O'Neal went berserk & shot a marijuana suspect 3 times in the back because O'Neal thought he looked like the Type that had defiled his daughter. The suspect, being led to a cell, had nothing whatsoever to do with the gang-rape. (The suspect was quoted from his hospital bed as saying that he could understand why O'Neal shot him because he, the suspect, was married & had a child of his own.)

Why must the enemy be the Law?

Current Myths:

The Police Dept.'s basement locker-room in the Jail building. On stone walls, battleship-grey, huge blow-ups photos of policemen killed in action.

Elephantine detail: a sergeant's kicked-in face, a lieutenant's slashed throat, a triad of bullets in a rookie's forehead, the bombed police car with mutilated bodies of two demolished officers

—They can see what they're up against, he said, before going on duty & they can see what they've avoided when they return from duty

Who is the enemy?

Revolutions create law in terms a time can understand.

"As part of his $7.50 treatment in a Cleveland men's hair salon, Benny Orzechowski, 18, wears a hair net, while his stylist—known as Frank the Razor—expertly puts the teased tresses into place."

LIFE: July / 65

COLLECTIVE YOUTH RITE Current Myths:

of Them: golems, huge shadow hulks that pass over our books as the True Word is readying to be seen:

of Them:

a pressure on the brain that menaces my freedom & binds me to economics; an electric shock to blind the eye when the eye most needs sight;

of Them:

a Mafia organizing the spirit into parts of a universal puppet-master schema (— the window's curtain ruffles back into place)

THEM (who)

destroyed plans for the car that ran on water, sunlight or air;

Them who didn't read Japan's acceptance of our A-Bomb ultimatum & who dropped the Bombs so that we could know the final power Them holds our collective destiny in;

Them — they are the terror of the unknown enemy that frustrates the ideals of men

Them who killed Kennedy, who killed Oswald;

keeping James Dean alive with Hitler in South America;

the Shaver Mystery;

who killed Robert Johnson, Harry Houdini, Kathy Fiscus, Richard Twardzik, Tom Mix, Albert Camus; Ernie Kovaks, Rimbaud, García Lorca, Jean Vigo, Theodore Roethke;

        O endless combinations!

THEM

whose institutions are knife-blades cutting into youth's speed muscles, hacking at their flanks

the enemy whose media is used to stop a person, to suffocate & diminish & finally eradicate that energy in a man's spirit & will;

dumping cancer into our food;

pesticides fluorides preservatives additives;

poisoning the earth destroying the birds and the fish swim in polluted streams;

wildlife dead not by multiple buckshot bullet punctures but of poisoning, laying stiff in ruts of sewerage litter garbage along state highways;

Them

who frustrate revolution, overwhelm revolt, by accepting it;

who open a window for Nijinsky to fly out of;

killers, spoilers, who contrive to control, arrange, manipulate;

Them serve the pedestal of fame; art's disorder; literature's disasters; missile-powered automation;

I thought no more was needed
Youth to prolong
Than dumb-bell and foil
To keep the body young.
O who could have foretold
That the heart grows old?
      from *A Song*: W. B. Yeats

skull-masked dream beasts torment youth with war maps tattooed on his forehead: the draft-notice:

Them sending messages of strategy to mothers whose daughters are being loved by young men who say poems when they talk; Them wants the young man's tongue in its trophy-room in a jar of glass for the tongue to clack against until the tongue says Yes;

Them who accept genius by refusing it; with ball-cutting clippers in unseen hands go to work making revolutions hang by the heels, disgraced;

THEM

whose power runs through before & after; cleaves out a principality from the halted runner's despair — blood from his smashed eyes mark the spot of his race's end;

THEM

the shield between man & rage against leaders who speak words out of Them's gall-bladder — standing before us on TV intoning a Texan drone, speaking vague words that turn into serene clouds fluffy & commanding as they drift o'er the brightest blue

hypnotizing us into a sleep (switching a switch, banging a gong, pressing a button) to alter mankind while we, in our trance, see only hillbilly seraphim & Green Pasture Negroes float by singing the National Anthem

—Don't you understand what I'm tryin to say,
Can't you feel the fear that I'm feelin today?
If the Button is pushed there's no runnin away.
There'll be no more to save with the world in a grave.
Take a look around yuh, boy, it's bound ta scare yuh, boy
. . .
And yuh tell me over and over and over again, my friend,
Ah you don't believe we're on the Eve of Destruction
[. . .]
Think of all the hate there is in Red China,
Then take a look around to Selma, Alabama.
You may leave here for four days in space,
But when you return it's the same old place.
The poundin of the drum, th' pride 'n' disgrace
          #4 / *Eve of Destruction*: Barry McGuire

WAR & DRAFTBOARD Current Myths:
Take all kinds of pills: forwards, backwards, coma pills, aspirin pills, sugar pills: all kinds & take 'em all at once & stay up for a few days & nights without bathing, shaving, combing, eating—drink lots of coffee, whiskey, wine (try pure alcohol — & try not to sleep)

then go for your Physical.   .

Tell Them you're a chronic bed-wetter; tell Them that you can't piss in public urinals;

eat a bushel of carrots & all that carotene will dye you skin carrot-yellow & the Army won't want you if you're yellow.

tell Them you're a Junkie;

tell Them that you really want to join soon as soon as possible because you love guns — all your life you've loved guns — everything about guns excites you: their feel, the weight of them, the butt, the shaft, the bore, — the trigger ah the trigger: how great a good trigger is to squeeze, to shoot that missile out into something — *any*-thing!

how urgent it is for you to be taken by the Army because you want to get out in the Viet

Nam jungle & start shooting, start killing them Jew Jap Niggers sonsabitches — kill anybody that moves! finally be able to kill real people with real bullets instead of just pretending like you used to do at home, peeping off rooftops with your telescopic sight; to the Jungle please with gun so me can kill O I love guns I'll oil my gun every day O the smell of gun-oil (I use Hoppe's Lubricating Oil)

O kill shoot — the trigger, the trigger, the trigger.

or eat peyote before you go (or take LSD or smoke lots of marijuana or a cake of hashish) or be yourself if your self is so alienatingly different than those other naked selfs waiting on line;

Go for your Physical dressed as a woman;

or be honest & try & know how honest you are & tell them why it's impossible for you to become a member of the Armed Forces

(Noble dying implies an ideal, a primal devotion to cause. This generation of young men before the Draft Board hardly know their mothers or fathers. How can they die for a country?

Some do it very easily

wearing an idea called Army/Navy/Marine/Air Force (each branch upholding specific comic-book notions easily adapted by the high school dropout or delusional hero—martyr)

into TV landscaped Vietnam they march

tribal blood thin but renewed by hasty boot-camp training meet vulgar death by bullet knife grenade

earlier writing brave letters to mothers & fathers; poems to sweethearts whose hearts will wear no widow's veil;

the band stops playing. The backdrop's rolled up. Terror's landscape affords no wide view. He smells every smell a fear-stricken body bleeds. Dying this way, blinders of futility shut out the lovely tropical malarial noon. Dying this way, he sees only futile unrelenting useless death embrace him & no God to share it with nor father to bless him nor mother to lead him to the father to the God to the beginning his birth demanded;

the slain young are fed back into the earth.

If a man does not know what he is living for, how can his death make sense?)

•

A schizoid empire (Robert Lindner once called America a Psychopathy) where lying, thieving & usury aid man in his quest for truth, love, order & justice.

Culture is a food for solitary confinement.

•

Saving myself is impossible without saving all.

72

•

How to step out of self
sealed between the two
sheets of pressed glass

when each forward step
deepens the rent
cleaves the tongue

song stopped by ears
stuffed with raven feathers
mouth filled with sea anemone

•

in newsreels high-divers in slow-motion backwards retrace their dive, return to the starting point at board's edge;

the knock-out punch in slow-motion & we all know that slow motion is created by using the camera's highest speed.

•

10 years ago the poets almost had it.

The Beat Generation image was the public's necessary scarecrow-placebo: Poets embrace fame ultimately to question it & to finally reject it.

It's a singer's world today. Tired of talk (or used to it) people wish to be sung to, to have the world re-named & re-ordered by singers & their songs.

•

"Jeff Newburg, 17, of Sparta, Wis. has given us a fad more cultural than marathon softball. He perched on the roof of a drive in restaurant and sang *I'm Henry the VIII, I am* for seven hours, 45 minutes. He quit after singing it 1001 times, saying he was tired of the whole thing."

Sports Illustrated: Aug. 9/65

PART 3

LITERATURE ! LITERATURE

Harper's Bazaar: April 1965 / *Seventeen*: May 1965
Bazaar: 141 pages of ads before getting the contents;
Seventeen: 117 pages of advertisements before the contents are revealed.

Both are primarily fashion magazines for the female[2] (& for the homosexual idealization of woman: hipless, breast-less, lean, boy-faced mannequins: sexless)

Seventeen is subtitled *America's Teenage Magazine*. It is an erotic primer that prepares the pubescent female to accept the strange Dachau of *Bazaar*.

Bazaar: Men without women create a working ideal of women without men: the models stand posed in leathers, plastics, helmets, hip-boots, thongs, space-suits, sailor-pants, paratrooper boots, leopard skin saris, shifts of imitation zebra skin;

stand in angular spread leg posture on legs invalid-thin: barren ladies with rocky faces, faces with the chill of stone in each polished line; — whose wounded lips (like fresh slashed wrists) are thin slits of a closed womb.

women without men make strange paper dolls for sad time worshippers to cut & paste on their collage lives.

·

Ownership, property, is the start of mass, of the burden. The man whose goods corrupt his heart lives in a house cluttered with unused (unrealized) objects whose importance is forgotten the moment of possession is consummated.

·

Like a man in drag: the Ultra-Blue Lady Clairol. Seduced by her vanity, she is the woman as masturbator without real need for man. She is all that men who dress like women seek to find: a fairy sketch of what is hateful in woman.

---

[2] They are trade journals, catalogues of advertisements for the manufactures represented & displayed within.—If they could, they'd let most people have the goddam things free,—I was told by a friend with complex knowledge of national magazines. (He had subscribed to hundreds of them repeatedly without ever paying for his subscriptions.) He said he was on his 5th year of *Life*, *Time*, *Prevention*, *High Fidelity*, *Motion Picture*, *Reader's Digest*, *Sports Afield*, *Post*, Reporter, *Hot Rod*, Etc.—"After a couple of months, after they stop sending you frantic bill—appeals, I pull out a post-free postcard from a magazine boosted from the Laundromat & re-subscribe.

Erinna; Sappho; Wonder-Woman
Cleopatra; Nyoka, Erinys
Hera; Ginger Rogers; Hero
the Amazons; Betty Hutton
Aimee Semple McPherson

    •

NOTHING WAS LEFT for
beneficiaries, nor for the
care of her mentally ill
mother, after debts and
taxes wiped out the $1
million estate of the late
actress Marilyn Monroe.

    •

Olive Thomas; Virginia Rappe
Jean Harlow; Lupe Velez
Marie Montez; Billie Holliday

Lilith, Circe, Astarte;
Isis, Mary, Sophia;
Gragon, Hecate, Kali;
MUSE   !   MUSE

    •

Celebrated for its use, her flesh is not the end of her but the beginning;
    start with Eve, the wonder of her birth, the dilemma made real, the mystery in her
dragon's mind which chose the serpent's song;
    Venus of Willendorf;
    creation, receiving, transforming man thru her patient art, of which his art is facsimile;
    earth her belly, moon her mind, the sun her heart,
    her spirit pervades the sacred earth, leads her man to magic combat
    the fury of her loins' work is creation.

—Hatty told Matty about a thing she saw had two big horns and a wooly Joe
Wooly bully, wooly bully, wooly bully
Wooly bully, wooly bully
                    #6 / *Wooly Bully*: Sam the Sham & The Pharaohs

THE PAIN & PLEASURE
OF LIFE'S MOST VIOLENT &
BEAUTIFUL SEXUAL EXPERIENCE
NATURAL CHILDBIRTH

    A film not for the weak
    An exciting and graphic view of a new life
        being thrust into the world.
    The torture — the love — the needs fulfilled.
        A collector's item.
1 — 100 ft. 8 mm $10.00
1 — 200 ft. 8 mm $20.00

        •

I'M 42+
and that's my bra size

        •

46 — 26 — 39

        •

RAISED SKIRT PHOTOS
Unretouched photos of amateur
models wearing nylons

        •

RUBBER GARMENTS

        •

Young girl from Lima, Peru
with 47" bust. Chris, the untamed,
bounces the TWIST

    •

The ghosts in *Bazaar* submit to the chill prodding of their private parts to create an image for women to ascend to — to imagine themselves looking chic & current ideal women clothed in the fashions of *Bazaar*.

—Fruggin' that fat away (below) — at Trude Heller's: Pamela Tiffin (the MOVIE STAR! dig?), Monti Rock III (the hairdresser: he rolls by day, rocks by night) — like they're wiggy. Threads making the bird: yellow silk dress, curved low, cooled with white ribbon lace that flakes out above the knee in a scallop. By Guy Douvier for the Arkins. About $110. At Woodward and Lothrop, Washington; Rich's, Atlanta; I. Magnin. Miss Tiffin will appear in Stan Vanderbeek's first feature film *A Dam Rib Bed*, and a pop-short, *His-Hers*, he is writing especially for her.

"Know anything about ROLLER DERBY? I see it on TV here every week looks like a whole amazing scene in itself — who the hell ARE those crazy—ass guys (& chicks) blasting each other over the rails at 40 mph & being hooted & screamed at by hordes of black leather JD's & old ladies with shopping bags like you see at wrestling matches? What do they do when they're not on? What kinda musics follow that?"

    from: a letter by Clark Coolidge

This is the Mouth
with the Message.

Young.
Fragile.
Faintly frosted.

Playing it
prim-and-proper.

But heartlessly
cool.

REVLON EXPOSES THE WORLDLY YOUNG INNOCENTS

& a couple of pages later Revlon advertises: the first shear-matte makeup for today's fair and fragile face . . . new TOUCH & GLOW crème soufflé makeup "suddenly faces go beautifully frail (not pale)— with a delicious new kind of makeup" followed, a few pages later, by Revlon's ad for frosted BLUSH-ON, "a little lift-of-color with a sprinkling of lights. . .delicious by day (and oh, the nights!)"

Peter Pan bras & girdles.

"This is the brush that puts on the blush that makes you look like you're falling in love!"

In the Boca Raton suit: a whipped-out mare who looks like Robert Helpmann

—now a fragrance you can FEEL / A VEIL OF ARPEGE / tonight I'll sleep in a Veil of Arpege / it clings —

"That men are afraid of women is not—despite the headlines—news. Men will always be afraid of women as long as patriarchy lasts, for the same reason millionaires will always tumble at the thought of revolution. The master fears the slave. The slave might revolt. There does not seem to be any reason why women should not enslave men. Men have enslaved women for ten thousand years."
                    from *Love & Death*: Legman

The April issue is the essence of The Scene . . . Andy Warhol photographs a glossary of currently correct words:

BAG: What you're hung up on. I'm in a Bogart bag . . . or a pizza bag.
SOMETHING ELSE: Very special. Dionne Warwick is something else.
ZERO COOL: Cooler than cool.

. . . OP ART & POP ART fashions: the ladies draped in optical illusions ("stripes (left) going absolutely out of sight 'in bamboo' & black—the tops in op fashion"). . . THE YOUNG AT ZERO COOL: "Wherever the action is in the space world of now, there is the new young man. With a toss of his long, extremely tossable hair, he makes Old Mr. Muscles —that crew-cut idol of the day before yesterday — look suddenly as square and wiped-out as the Hupmobile. The man of the hour is a boy in his twenties . . . Today he seriously collects colognes, perfumes, powders, shave creams, and shampoos. Tomorrow, almost surely, he will order unguents for his complexion, masks for his circulation and — who knows? make-up for his . . . beauty."

                    U.S. CIGARETTE WARNING / GOES UP IN SMOKE
                    United Press Washington
                    "The Agriculture Department said yesterday U.S. smokers are
                    using more cigarettes now than they did before the smoking and

health report of January 11, 1964.

The department estimated cigarette consumption for fiscal year, 1965, which ends today, at a record of 533 billion.

This is about 24 billion cigarettes more than were consumed in 1963-64 when there was a short-term decline in smoking following the Surgeon-General's report.

The department said the estimated fiscal 1965 figure is 16 billion above the previous fiscal year high of 1962—63."

fashions by Courreges: a model in a shrunken play suit wears chalk white sunglasses with minute slits in them to see the large grey world drag by

SHIRT: Sam. Boss. *That's a shirt skirt.*
STOKE: Boss. *White stockings?—that's stoke.*

an article by Tom Wolfe: timed, timely data gushed forth in foamy folds much like custard pushed out of a machine, piled into a Pop Art ice cream cone; custard you've got to eat right away or it melts into a thin yellow stream;

of the current, the immediate, but where is the timeless? (Ah the snipers speak large words, & ask large questions, & poets hide behind billboards living on rooftops with telescopic high power rifles stalk about like chimneysweeps, wait for order to order itself & tell them when to cease fire)

Only the struggle for order is timeless.

MAN, These computers Swing!
For a computer analysis of
what you should look for in
your ideal mate, it's Com-
puter A Go Go. Box 2818, SF

America! land of everyone's democratic despair found in a magazine! Whitman's rosebush cloud finally parts to rain upon the desert. All can find their dream before them.

Cunt removed, she's clothed in the debris of that operation. The bones remain. An idea of woman stands in stiff, strange poses, archaic woodcut stances.

4 full—page photos of

1) Henry Geldzahler — "a pop art personality"
2) Jasper Johns — "painstaking (painter) of dart boards, flags & numbers"
3) Robert Rauschenberg — "& colleague Alex Hay"
4) Bob Dylan — "the teenagers' troubadour" looking like a young Cocteau in belted suede coat, tight black pants, limp leather boots, a tie—less wide collar, standing on wet cobbles

with unfurled hair applied to his skull like wild sumi-e brush strokes

Two full page color reproductions of:

1) a Pop-Art painting by Roy Lichtenstein used in conjunction with a plug for Deuces Wild lipstick "Mauve, Red, Orange or Cocoa, applying a coat of clear yellow or white for highlight only to the lower lip!"
2) a sculpture by George Segal, W*oman Washing Her Feet* — "the sandals, which are an integral part of the sculpture . . . by Mademoiselle. About $21. At Neiman-Marcus."

The 'artist's circle'. His art competes with advertisement. Pop-Art: Ouroboros.
Full-page & quarter-page photos of Ringo Starr — "perhaps the best of the Beatles" — bare torso, crowned with laurel;
Full-page photo of Paul McCartney — "cosmic, yes, yes, yes, sends the faithful into orbit!" — in a space suit looking Heavenward into the klieg light to his left;
A list of Underground movies & movie-makers ("the name Underground Movie coined by Vanderbeck for the controversial new American film trend")

". . . the Ad Lib is where the In Crowd goes. Nureyev in one corner. Ringo in another, holding Maureen's hand, jerking in his seat to the beat of 'The In Crowd.' Lord Suffolk, Lord Rudolph Russell, Lord Hartford . . . Baroness Von Thyssen . . . Viscount Dunluce . . . Vidal Sassoon . . . the Marchioness of Tavistock, Prince Radizwill . . . Tiger Morse, Margot Fonteyn, Lord Plunkett, the Maharance of Jaipur . . . Nobody stares . . . a quiet club for members only . . . no tourists. There's air there, the greatest records, room to dance. All making the scene together: the world of pop, the theatre, photographers, private people and private public people . . . the walls are black glass. In pinky candle shine, half quenched by the dark underwater light, girls are beautiful — terrible. Every time you go, new ones come in — darling, pretty and young. 'Delicious,' the young men say about them and their clothes. They are like children, ad-libbing, dressing-up, in a ravishing excitement of discovering how they can change their looks, which will never happen again,"
    Harper's Bazaar: Apr. 1965

There, a lexicon, a guidebook to attitudes, names, & ideals.
Fragile testament of temporal faiths.
Additional photos of young English Lords & Ladies who look like wolves & whippets

"Martin: I was mistaken when I set out to destroy Church and Law. The battle we have to fight is fought out in our own mind. There is a fiery moment, perhaps once in a life time, and in that moment we see only the thing that matters. It is in that moment that great battles are lost and won, for in that moment we are a part of the host of Heaven."
    from *The Unicorn From The Stars*: W. B. Yeats

Part 4

Seventeen: —

Times go by so fast. The code still unbroken.

Those left will be those who could sit still, wait, & abide with faith in their natural ability to grow.

Spine arched, pelvis thrust forth, breasts pushed up, wearing a 2 piece bathing-suit — the halter & panties both tied to their centers with white shoelace

"The girl with the beautiful mouth . . ." Her face looking at you is held in the hands of a man drawing her lips to his. To witness the ad is to partake in a popular tradition of being both voyeur & lover . . . "She has it made with New Clairol Lipstick."

On the go . . . bongo boards
riding the surf. Cycling with him.
Learning guitar.
In the know . . . European schools . . .
007, Master Spy. Sing along
with Lesley Gore . . . catch
those Keane eyes!
Letting the New Young Look show
with patterned stockings and posh
high boots, false eye lashes and
sleek slack suits. A-line skirts and
antique jewels, or wheat jeans
and tennis shoes.
But most of all an Aware One is. . .
AWARE OF HER HAIR!

Speed stopped & you can step inside the photograph & live there.

When they're asked they will say that they don't really believe in Beach Blanket Bingo but they'll go see it because they can only disbelieve what they see.

"You have in Darlene!"

"It's the berries! / six crashing new colors / to swing your Spring" . . . Resting elbow deep in artificial strawberries, boysenberries, apple-berries, is a young lady in a strapless red dress (movie starlet of the 40's) looking not exactly at me or into me because her eyes are transfixed. In her hand she holds a half-eaten wooden fake berry (held like a teacup, her pinkie arched elegantly wearing a pearl, sapphire, ruby Yvonne De Carlo ring) her mouth is open to display her tongue tip: pink triangle between her brilliant teeth;

Eeeeek! My complexion's in a shambles!
(Bound to happen with all this excitement.)
That's why I smooth on Angel Face . . .

Materia newly minted: instant stuff. No panic, no patina on relics left unsold. No time for nostalgia unless the consumer is buying nostalgia & then there's ample marketplaces for good times gone. (The re-bound sounds on the radio dip into a repertoire of records rarely older than 6 years.)

He can't get you out of his mind when
Wind song whispers your message
What else are you doing?

Most days I go to the studio and talk to people, pose for publicity pictures, read scripts, see the hairdresser. A lot of things.

> MENDOTA (Ill.) — (AP) — Devotees of rags-to-riches author Horatio Alger, Jr. plan to organize the Horatio Alger Society of America.
> Students of the noted American author, whose 130 works, written 1864-1899, have sold millions of books, will be attending from a score of states, from Massachusetts to Utah and from Minnesota to Tennessee.

Shipboard: sailboat, yacht: the *Seventeen* models model FASHIONS AFLOAT ("All Under $20") — grouped together, smiling bright virgin-sweet smiles of the clean sun-washed just-showered young maidens chosen to illustrate that which is perfect in puberty: in the pictures erotically hip to hip clutching at prows, poles, ropes, ballast

> SKIMPS, SKOOT SUITS
> A SKINNY, A SKAMP!
> SOAKERS AND SAND SUITS
> SUN SMOCKS!

they're girls of a familiar high school torment — who beguiled my awakened eyes when they passed by as if on rollers, so easy did they whip their butts down noisy halls;

neat, stately, her beauty sets her apart. Her course already set. She symbolized to me the prefabricated Teen Queen dream who ultimately frustrated me because no matter how useful the vision of her, it was impossible for me to desire her — she was like one of the ladies cluttering Fitzgerald's Great American Country Club: unobtainable, somehow lethal with unspoken demands & hungers & paralyzed by the large ignorance alive in Beautiful

People of the American middle class;

today's Barbie Dolls resemble them: mythic teenage girl made real, then manufactured into a doll to bear her image, then the doll used as a model for the real: — how we are what we worship & how we worship what we are;

a Barbie Doll culture: a whole family of dolls with scale-sized clothing & variegated accoutrements: purses, combs, belts, wigs, curlers, telephone, underwear, a Jaguar for Barbie's sexless boyfriend Ken. Etc.

Dear Problems Page,
Every day at the bus stop I see a
beautiful girl who is just my type.
I smile at her but she never smiles back.
How can I attract her interest?
Tormented

Dear Tormented,
Maybe your smile just hasn't got what
some other smiles have. Try chewing
DENTYNE CHEWING GUM

— They were rich kids, a townsman said, describing how 7 youths in a new car pulled a girl off a busy street & took her into a field to rape her continuously for 3 hours & then deposit her in a state of shock in front of a drive-in.

Archetypal woman: her division in the dream cells of our collective workings—her forms fill the cultural psyche — a brush fire — a dark landscape of wild hills, labyrinths, unheard-of mazes & circuits — vales & forests, elemental glens — her faces in the air like pollens & hydrocarbons — faces shaped from air's wires into formal structure — instant of transfusion — signal in the mind — phantom of sun watched too long — a red emblem;

their myth is the myth to be made of them. It is connected to maidens who dance a ring around attic-black vases & on the televised stages of SHINDIG or HULABALOO.

The girls of *Seventeen* are not the mannequins of *Bazaar*. But they are as untouchable. A man wouldn't want to undress a *Bazaar* model for fear she might be a man or might splinter his hands. Nor would he want to have a sexual relation with a *Seventeen* model. Though they are there in color before you lying on shipboard, hip snapped towards you, neck line, flank line, breasts — their readiness is also terror: maiden, nymph, sylph — they live in the eyes, the mind, of man as a timeless moment, a girl entering womanhood — they are before you strangely like sisters & to seduce them would be to violate their immortality & tribal law.

1. A younger child will watch anything that an older one will watch.

2. An older child will not watch anything, a younger child will watch.

3. A girl will watch anything a boy will watch.

4. A boy will not watch anything a girl will watch.

5. In order to catch your greatest audience, zero-in on a 19-year-old male.

> SAM ARKOFF'S PETER PAN SYNDROME:
> Arkoff along with Jim Nicholson run American International Pictures who produce teenage beach-gang type movies. Their 1st big hit was *I Was A Teenage Werewolf* (1957)

DIVE
    INTO
        SUMMER

Enjoy every single one of those sun-swept days, the velvety nights. Be confident, comfortable with the cool, clean fresh protection of TAMPAX

for the maiden's first moon-drawn blood saturated in the cotton phallus inserted in her vagina; — or soaked into a cotton hand between her legs; *Seventeen* features fashions, sanitary napkins, brassieres, girdles & skin creams primarily; many ads for silverware & crockery appeal to the marriage-bent teenager (*Are you the kind of girl the boy next door gives Royal Worcester to? even though he doesn't know where his next $79 is coming from ...*) & engagement & wedding rings & the poetry of advertising's need to sell the impossible over & over again:

Go girls go-go for the neatest,
nittiest shape you've ever
been in. Treo shapes up a gentle shape,
young, lithe and lean with
rounded
natural
curves in lyrically lovely
lightweight basics to
underscore today's
swinging silhouette.

     • • •

frugging frantically,
monkeying madly
or whatever
"in" shapemaker
takes you in & shapes you out
lovingly!
yeah . . . yeah

(shown: Proportioned derriere-shaping panty girdle with lacy cuffs & "Cheers" push-up, deep plunge bra.) Bards watch your arts, your times, & your tempers.

My childhood sweetheart lived around the corner. I went over there one afternoon to make her laugh, to bug her, to make my presence known. She was on the cement front porch standing in the center of a circle formed by her four best girl-friends. They were whispering, incanting, about her first menstruation. Uttering whispered warnings & prophecies about bizarre pregnancies, weird homunculi, unaccounted for protrusions, obstructions;

I sat away from them, looking at the street, a parked Packard sedan, listening to the sounds of a rite. How different my sweetheart looked in the circle's center, her voice unknown to my memory. In sequence, each of her four girl-friends would turn to look at me & then, quickly, return to the chanting of initiatory hymns. Such strange looks. Not being able to move, I sat there kicking the stoop with the back of my heel & feeling a peculiarly male inadequacy.

"Can we not see that it matters not whether a man has learned of the Path from the teachings of Krishna or of the Buddha, or of Mohammed or Zoroaster, or of the Christ, — provided he but set his foot upon that Path, it is all one to our common Father."
from: *Fragments Of A Faith Forgotten*: G. R. S. Mead

In my 15th summer I took a private trip to that block in Brooklyn hoping to see her again, hoping to return to a remembered Eden &, because growing had been hard that month, I thought that I would stay there forever with my old friends. She was the only one left who remembered me.

Wearing a tight striped T-Shirt & a tight black skirt, she asked me into her bedroom to see her books & watched me nervously chain smoke Viceroy Cigarettes. (— Look, she later told her mother, — Look at David smoking! As if that were the true meaning of my presence there that afternoon. Her mother graciously tolerated my disguises. She offered me a cup of coffee. — Black, I said, squashing out the cigarette.)

On her bed was a white chenille bedspread. She opened up a cardboard clothes closet & dug out a pile of paperback books stashed in shoeboxes. *God's Little Acre, The Amboy Dukes, I, The Jury.*

(We used to read through blue volumes of her *Jr. Britannica* set when we were in the 5th grade. She was an honor-student. — O you're so damned smart! she'd scream at my 10-year-old erudition. Even then I had a finely developed instinct for rhetoric. Yet she got the good grades. I was good in talking my way out of bad ones.)

—Y'know how to fuck a girl?
—No. How d'you fuck a girl, Freddie? He looked at me with dark knowledge
—Y'stick your prick in her hole & pee in her
—Really?

91

—Why should l lie?

The Chinese Room   *Dim View*   *The Sling & The Arrow*   *A Report On The Kinsey Report* —her secret collection of paperbacks spread before me, (honor-student, flag-bearer, valedictorian of P.S. 232; who once played Malaguena on the upright in her living room for me) — she asked me if I wanted to feel her breasts, moving to me, licking her lips & removing powderblue-rimmed glasses

•

Current ephemera clots the newsstands with colorful covers overwhelmed with typography:

WHY I CAN'T MARRY by JODY McCREA
GEORGE HARRISON: "MY SUICIDE PACT"
FORGIVE US MR. GILARDI . . . BUT DID YOU KNOW ABOUT ANNETTE & FRANKIE?
           RINGO'S NIGHT OF LOVE
ROLLING STONES' BIGGEST FAILURE . . . WHO IS SCARING CONNIE STEVENS? . .
BRITISH GROUPS ARE DEAD
     THE BEATLES BECOME SNEAKY SNOBS . . . HEADED FOR THE TEEN FAN JUNKPILE . . . GARDNER McKAY'S STRANGE LOVE . . . WHAT THE BEACH GIRLS WEAR TO BED . . . IS SEX BREAKING UP THE BEATLES? . . . CAN THE EVERLY BROTHERS DO IT AGAIN? . . . IS BOB DYLAN JOHN LENNON? . . . EXTRA! THE MONSTERS ARE HERE! ! . . . CONFIDENCE MADE THE SEEKERS . . . ELVIS IS STILL KING!
TEEN PIN-UPS . . . TEEN TALK . . . THE TEEN SET
TEEN WORLD . . . TEEN LIFE . . . TEEN SCRAPBOOK
KEEN TEEN . . . TEEN . . . TEEN SCENE

The magazines are a dead-letter file of myth-seed, bad reporting, passion, loyalty & the victimizing of the passionate & the loyal with (often) fraudulent contest-offers & misnamed products[3];
—Thank heavens for *Teen Pin-Ups* ! ! ! You really make me feel so much closer to "my" Beatles . . . when I saw "The Beatles — Here's What Scares Us To Death," tears actually came to my eyes. I could barely keep from whimpering like a baby . . . sometimes I think that *Teen Pin-Ups* is the only mag that can make me really happy. Unless by some miracle I married Ringo!
SONG HITS . . . HIT PARADER

---

[3] "Peter and I talk about accuracy and honesty in magazines. 'A magazine once had a contest and for a prize they offered one of my sister Jane Asher's pocketbooks with a note from her inside. The first Jane knew of the contest was when she opened the magazine. On the note, they'd copied Jane's signature from a letter she had once sent them. It was an angry letter.'"
On The Town with Peter & Gordon / SONG HITS: October, 1965

92

SONGS & STARS . . . KYA BEAT
RAVE . . . SMASH . . . INGENUE

—After Rick Nelson got married, lots of my friends gave up on him. But I will love him eternally. My room is plastered from ceiling to floor with pix of his beautiful face that I cut out from your great mag

The news is no news: tentative, vague & repetitive. Enough to allow the imagination material to create with.

Along with stories & photos of the dominant heroes are stories & photos of regional Beatle facsimiles. Smiling too stiffly, they hold their guitars in a way to make you realize that they haven't finished paying for them & that this Professional Photo better score them meaningful gigs. Faces stamped from an essential die of tragedy; faces whose shape & character are shapeless & characterless; faces whose contours bear some resemblance to the archetypes but not enough to act as their replacement or substitute.

The Pet Milk label makes clear that point where all the faces & words go.

INTIMATE QUESTIONS ANSWERED BY LESLEY GORE
—Was singing your first ambition?
—I've wanted to be a recording star since I was three years old.
& JODY McCRAE
—Have you any secret wish?
—To marry a Princess.

Song starts in the body's lair & works its way of the body in a way not unlike *Kundalini Shakthi*, or serpent power.

Invisible connections unthread the mind from mystery-flesh that responds & moves to an ecstasy abruptly stopped by the record's end.

The announcer's voice:
—Knock. Knock.
—Who's there?
—Ringo.
—Ringo who?
—Now that he's married you see you've forgotten him.

Song is offered by non-singers: basketball players, boxers, baseball players, movie-&-TV-actors. All want to sing a song into the dark of the great lair. They wish their sound to go to its depths & ripple great waters. Song to sink to the sea's bottom as a relic, sea-glazed, waiting future discovery.

"Papago songs are handed down from singer to singer more carefully than were the epics of

Homer. A man dreams his own songs, and he gives them to his son; but before he was born, there was already a body of magic by which the ancestors ruled the world."
from: *Singing For Power* by Ruth Underhill (UC Press; 1938)

To make song is to forget speech.

The magazines, books, newspapers, roar off the presses. Fill up the newsstand racks. When the next issue is printed they are taken off the stands. The returned copies are useless unless re-used by distributors for wrapping paper. Next month: new titles, new headlines ("Intimate confessions of your favorite stars"). History is news. Gossip.

—The word these days is "pshaw," pronounced shaw!

" . . . while the police have their place in society . . . this magazine doesn't think that policemen should vent their rage on teenagers in the form of using outright brutality. Their job is to restrain . . . not beat, push, club or run helter-skelter into teen-groups with riot-trained horses. Every day we read about teenagers being injured, beat up, shot at . . . all this at the very hands of the police who are supposed to be our friends. This kind of police state . . . with all its brutality doesn't belong in America . . . and steps should be taken to stop it. Teenagers who are victims should report these incidents to their parents . . . write letters to their mayor . . . and to this magazine . . . this is not a world in which (brutality) belongs."
from: *Keen Teen* / April 1965

An unusual editorial for a teenage magazine. They are, with rare exception, seemingly published by one company, edited by the same editor. Their editorial policy maintains a pseudo-naïf pose of insular wordlessness that attempts to create a narcotic ambivalence to anything other than myth-making & selling products most directly associated with the principal idols & gods. The manufacture of teen goods is an adult enterprise. The adult lack of understanding & inherent fear of the consumer must be the same fear a white businessman must feel each day when he opens his shop in Harlem.

Self-defensive contempt & fear can only simplify. It *teaches* consumption, planning artificial consumer commandments into the pubescent nerve-center.

Revolution begins with words, with the sound of them being stated or sung.

Then the sight of the leader; his heroic visage.[4]

" . . . For those who think the Beatles are good musicians, you've got a big hole between your ears. Not one of the boys can read a good sheet of music (sic?) . . . John and George using the chord system . . . with Paul playing a four string bass that can be off half the time without anybody knowing . . . "
from: *Keen Teen*: April, 1965

---

[4] Soviet photos of Stalin with wrinkles & dyeing airbrushed out.

No straight line out. All assumptions are circular.

"For a while I would just like to sit in the shade with a glass of wine in my hands and watch the people dance."
Adlai Stevenson: 2 days before his death

Part 5

We are witness to the emergence of a song-culture, an instant tradition of city minstrelsy made from blood mixed in England's rivers with molten gold out of America's bladder.

It is the folk music of cities, the tribal singing of American youth.

It's the news of city dreaming, the dreams made from news.[5]

These hymns are unrelentingly moral & self-protective, as all hymns are.

It is the sound of raging cities whose night-fall brings monsters to balance the dead-eyed angels that guide the day race home.

All superficial stances, dances, gestures of potency, hunger for mother's blessing, woman's mysteries, concocted by alchemic bards of industry in recording studios & rushed hot to the market.

It is a music that defines the heart & bounds of the nation's trivial imagination; it's a music easily used against itself & easily forgotten.

It's a music that one day is new & the next day old. It's a music that declines its time & cannot transcend it.

RECORD INDUSTRY Current Myths:
The cosmical production company that produced a 3½ minute long record of silence.

The songs are songs of the sublime middle-class youth who own them, consume them, dream through them & ornament their thinking with them. The songs affirm the tenets of the middle-class laws. Even the so-called protest songs affirm the middle-class ethic. For instance

She had a bad childhood when she was very young[6]
So don't judge her too badly·.
She had a schizophrenic mother who worked in the gutter,
Would have sold herself to the Devil gladly.
What a sad environment in a bug-ridden tenement
And when they can't pay the rent
It's cause their father was out getting sicker.
Oh the stone's been cast
And blood's thicker than water
And the sins of a family fall on the daughter
At the age of 16 she'd been around more than any girl over 30

---

[5] Sidewalk Surfing. The Space Walk. Ballad of the Green Beret. The Jolly Green Giant. We Love You Beatles. Ballad of Mike Hammer. Eve of Destruction. 19th Nervous Breakdown. I Fought The Law. Etc.

[6] A few years ago on TV on the Steve Allen Show there was a stooge named Dayton Allen whose opening greeting was: Why not? From the 1st line to the last, this song could possibly been ghosted by Dayton Allen.

—And the high IQ's who condemned her knew
She was a product of poor heredity.
The Devil is open to all of us.
Heaven selects a precious few.
It takes an inside pull to get Gabriel to make an angel out of you,
One can't live a lie and expect to die with your soul in Paradise
You gotta pay the price like you oughta
And the sins of a family fall on the daughter.
from: The Sins Of A Family / written by P. F. Sloan

400 pop-singles in a week. Enough dream-fuel to turn the mind into cottage cheese. Jam all the circuits with musical suet.

The songs are concerned with love. Even most of the protest songs protest familial despair induced by love's lack. Everyone who is young wants to be understood first by their parents. A Biblical hunger to be blessed by the father & the mother.

American song, our immediate folk song, is easily divided into specific regional sounds: Hollywood, Nashville, Chicago, Detroit. These cities are the major song-centers producing the majority of pop singles & lp records. Each city has its recognized sound.

•

DETROIT, the Motor City, is an echo-chamber of assembly lines roaring in a fury of sound within sound: a black electronic maze whose minotaurs are 3 girls from a low-income housing project, The Supremes;

their voices on record move into the ear then vanish — baritone sax there, then gone, winged, honking thru the haze of over-dubbed orchestral sounds — the drummer's constant off-beat drum-rim cracks in a cavern like sniper fire — the voices come & go as voices heard in Visions: aether soundings that appear, fragment into parts that divide to finally disperse into the great void of all sound singing

—Love Love Love Love
Hey, hey
Oh, oh
Hey, hey

DETROIT, home of Motown, Tamla, Gordy,[7] manufacture a grey sound based on assumptions made by black & white clearly integrated in their efforts to capture the

---

[7] Besides The Supremes other artists associated with the Detroit record Industry are: Marvin Gaye, Smokey Robinson & The Miracles, Martha & The Yandellas, The Marvelettes, The Four Tops, The Temptations, Etc.

marketplace. The white man's over-arranged background music to hold the black man's song, to submerge it, baptize it, scrub it clean. The black man's willingness to advocate the white romantic delusional idealism. (We will have Doris Day playing the lead in the Billie Holliday Story.) Both races fully integrated in the common lust for freedom bought by economic triumph. A dial-tone in the minds of men.

•

LOS ANGELES (HOLLYWOOD & SEA-SWEPT ENVIRONS) is the sound of Pacific surf turned into whipped-cream: Freeway music of teenage sub-dolphins who loiter on beaches or in drive-ins, driving sports cars, hot rods, motorcycles, scooters, whose girls are legendary beauties who litter California beaches until the eye gets bored with such repetitive abundance;

an orange-juice culture with ritual sports (surfboarding: "The Sport of Ancient Hawaiian Kings & Princes") — sea-imprisoned music sung by youth facing the end of the American continent with pride & fear.

The dream's medusa mother here with wings outspread in sunset brilliance above the movie lots, tv lots, record studios.

From dark city boxes in the Eastern rockpile the spirit travels West to the great foamrubber Hollywood: the tower facing the Orient with millions of long-haired princesses banging their braids down the walls for millions of long-haired princes to grab ahold of & scale styrene walls;

& embrace before a TV set & phone a Chinese restaurant to deliver the Dragon for their dinner; surrounded by middle-class forts & valleys, Hollywood is the middle-class's highest Utopian reality: the imagination created Hollywood for the old to uphold as they sit on bus benches in the sun & for the young to ignore in their woodys headed for the beach tossing empty Country Club cans out the window;

Bard of the ocean-front, the California teenager, of teenage materialism, is Brian Wilson, leader of The Beach Boys. He writes a good 90% of the songs the group performs.

His songs sing the glory of the California teenager's white middle class Nirvana in exacting words that describe the bliss of objects. Like Chuck Berry, Wilson is often a vehicle-bard. In fact, his major song subjects are love& flight. His sense of the California teenager's scene & dream is precise. Many of his songs deal with drag-racing, surf-boarding.

—*It's not a big motorcycle,*
   Just a groovy little motor bike
   [. . .]
   It climbs the hill like a mattress
   'Cause my Honda's built real light.
   When I go into the turn,
   Oh hang on tight.

I better turn on the lights
So we can ride my Honda tonight,
1st gear, it's all right.
2nd gear, hold me tight.
3rd gear, hang on tight,
Faster, it's all right!
                    — Little Honda.

His love songs are written with romantic realism;

—Sometimes l have a weird way of showin my love
And I always expect her to know what I'm thinkin of
(She knows me, she knows me)
I treat her so mean,
I don't deserve what I have
And I think that she'll forget just by makin her laugh
But she knows me, knows me so well
[. . .]
I get jealous of other guys
And then I'm not happy 'till make her break down and cry.
When I look at other girls it must kill her inside,
But it'd be another story if she looked at the guys.
She knows me, knows me so well.
                    — She Knows Me

Or this romantic statement of fact:

—On the beach you'll find them there
In the sun and salty air.
The girls on the beach are all within reach
If you know what to do.
How we love to lie around girls with tans of golden brown.
The sun in her hair, the warmth in the air
On a summer day.   .
As the sun dips out of sight: couples on the beach at night.
                    — The Girls On The Beach

Or:

—Sittin in my car outside your house:
Member when you spilled Coke all over your blouse.
T-shirts, cut-offs and a pair of thongs.
We've been havin fun all summer long.
Miniature golf and Hondas in the hill;
When we rode horses it gave us a thrill.
Every now and then we hear our song.
            — All Summer Long

When he deals with the comradeship of the pubescent male (and their sexual/love/worship of the automobile: *This Car of Mine; Cherry, Cherry Coupe; Our Car Club* — Etc.) Wilson details limits in the mind & heart of middle-class California youth:

—I get around, I get around, I get around
I'm a real cool head.
I'd make a real good friend.
I'm gettin bugged drivin up and down the same old strip.
I gotta find a new place where the kids are hip.
[. . .]
We always (his buddies) take my car because it's never been beat.
[. . .]
None of the guys go steady because it wouldn't be right
To leave your best girl at home on a Saturday night.
            — I Get Around

& there's Wilson's hymn to the drive-in movie:

—Every time I have a date,
There's only one place to go:
That's the Drive-In
It's such a groovy place to talk and maybe watch a show
Down at the Drive-In.
[. . .]
If the windows get fogged, you'll have to take a breath
or the cat dressed in white'll scare you both to death
A big buttered popcorn and an extra-large Coke,
A few chili dogs and, man, I'm goin' broke!
[. . .]

Don't sneak your buddies in the trunk
'Cause they might get caught
And it'd look kinda stupid bein' chased around the lot
At the Drive-In.
                    — *The Drive In*

"That goes to show you. They don't have anything really different. They're just regular guys. They have a great sound. But, personally, they're just like anybody else right out there in the audience."

>   Jan Berry (of Jan & Dean — a group that sounds so much like the Beach Boys that it's easy to confuse the two groups' sound.)

The Beach Boys is a quintet composed of three brothers Wilson (Brian, Dennis & Carl), one cousin & one neighbor. Their vocal sound is distinct & utilizes intricate vocal harmonies & counterpoint.

Brian Wilson, the leader, produces all of their record sessions.

"A sociologist might say I am trying to generate a feeling of social superiority. I live with my piano and I love to make records that my friends like to hear."

—What's your opinion of the European music scene?
—There aren't enough young people in the business, replies Brian.
—What's your criteria for success?
—Record sales and screams.

With the face of a child who has overslept, Wilson produces records for other artists too. He is 24 years old.

From their first hit in 1961, the Beach Boys have refined what is recognized as their Sound. All of their recordings, chronologically endured, sound essentially the same. The content of the songs remain the same. The Beach Boys will not grow up & exemplify the Peter Pan syndrome that holds so much of America in firm throttle. In their candy-striped short-sleeved shirts & modestly tight pants they will fight back inevitable natural destinies, holding firm to the Dumbo feather.

—Hey, Earl. Get your camera ready! (Dennis Wilson) called.
—I'm gonna run up to the Wall and spit on it just to show those dirty Communist finks what I think of them!

•

CHICAGO is the pit, the mid-city, whose darkness burns with its ghetto-jewels.[8] Chicago is black.

—Meanwhile tourists are beginning to drive through Watts collecting souvenirs in the rubble & debris left by the three day rioting while National Guardsmen walk the streets with rifles ready

Chicago's glory is Chicago's despair. Home of slaughterhouses & the jungle-dealings of the oppressed, its music, for the most part, is popular only to the Negro & is an extension of the Negro country blues tradition. It has been tremendously influential especially in Europe where imported Chicago blues have performed to packed concert halls of attentive audiences. Groups like the Rolling Stones, Beatles: Animals, Etc., are always the first to acknowledge their tremendous debt to the many groups first recorded in Chicago.

"I have a funny feeling. I have a feeling that a White is going to get at it and really put over the blues. But I don't know whether they can deliver the message. I know they feel it, but I don't know if they can deliver it!"
Muddy Waters: Rhythm & Blues / July 1964

One of the most influential single Negro performers on the music of today is Chuck Berry. As a composer, guitarist & performer, Berry has been a major influence on both the sound & content of today's popular music — &, ironically, Berry is one of the few Negro songwriters to write songs to & about the white middleclass teenagers[9].

Berry is black & he is white. His songs are a blending of both worlds, yet they are not grey. His words & music do not, by the blending, represent a compromise as so many of the

---

[8] Chicago has held onto or let go of such major city blues singers, seminal musicians, as Howlin' Wolf, Sonny Boy Williamson, Muddy Waters, Little Walter, Jimmy Reed. It is one of the primal cities in the development of rhythm & blues. It is the home of Chess & Checker Records whose list is a history of significant recorded urban music; a roll-call of major Negro artists whose work laid the foundation for many less-original musicians to build their fortunes upon.

[9] The pervasive influence of Berry can be heard, for instance, in the Beach Boys early instrumental stylings & in the verbal extensiveness employed by Brian Wilson in many of his lyrics. (See above). The Beatles' version of Berry's *Roll Over Beethoven*, is instrumentally so much like Berry that when you hear the first few bars; you could swear that Chuck Berry was playing guitar instead of George Harrison. Almost every major white rock n' roll band plays at least one Chuck Berry composition. & last week I saw an album of Chuck Berry compositions played by Jim & Jesse McReynolds, a well-known country bluegrass band with liner notes written by Berry. (I have recently heard an album of Beatles' songs played by Chet Atkins, the great Nashville guitarist, with liner notes written by George Harrison.)

blendings inevitably do. Berry is in his mid-30s & he has a wit & sense of irony that can be razor-sharp in its work, especially in his Teen Age America type of songs.

—*They furnished off an apartment with a 2-room Roebuck sale;*
The coolerator was crammed with TV dinners & ginger ale.
[. . .]
They had a hi-fi phono:
Boy, did they let it blast.
700 little records: all Rock, Rhythm and Jazz
But when the sun went down,
The rapid tempo of the music fell,
[. . .]
They bought a souped-up jitney,
T'was a cherry red '53.
                   — *You Never Can Tell*

        (The literature of pop-song lyrics must have many volumes of songs dealing with Teen Age brides & grooms. Perhaps the first popular song on the subject was (They Tried To Tell Us We're) Too Young sung by Nat King Cole c. 1952. Teenage marriage songs either live happily ever after or die morality-play deaths.)

    Or the imaginative version of escape, an ideal teenage idyll:

—*And in our little rendezvous*
We'll have a beautiful wedding day
[. . .]
And I'll build a spaceship with a heavy payload
And we'll go beep, beep, beep
Way out in the wide open blue
[. . .]
We'll take a basket, a shortwave radio
Tune in on the record shows all over the whole wide world
Send a signal back to mom and dad from me and you
                   — *Our Little Rendezvous*

    The irony & immediacy of this situation is indicative of Berry's wit:

—*No particular place to go*
So we parked way out on the Kokomo.
The night was young and the moon was gold

So we both decided to take a stroll.
Can you imagine the way I felt,
I couldn't unfasten her safety belt?
                    — *No Particular Place to Go*

Speed & motion are constant themes in Berry's songs;

—*As I was motivatin' over the hill,*
I saw Maybelline in a Coupe de Ville
Cadillac a-rollin' on a open road.
Nothin' out-runnin' my V-8 Ford.
Cadillac doin' about 9 5.
Bumper to bumper, rollin' side to side.
Cadillac and Ford up to l04.
Ford got too hot and wouldn't do no more.
It got cloudy and started to rain.
I tooted my horn for the passing lane—
The rain water poured all under my hood.
I knew that wasn't doin' my motor good.
                    — *Maybelline*

—*Work out bobby soxer*
You can wiggle like a whimsical fish
Go, go, bobby soxer
[. . .]
Bobby soxer dancing but she keeps a-peeping at the stand.
Bobbysox got a crush on the Beatle in the bobby band.
Love-bug sure gonna bite her if the Beatle even waves his hand.
[. . .]
Twist on bobby soxer, but don't forget the bobby rule.
'Gettin' late bobby soxer and the teacher teaching you is cruel
And tomorrow morning, bobby soxer, you'll be back in school.
Go, go, bobby soxer.
                    — *Go Bobby Soxer*

—*Well, early in the mornin'*
And I'm givin' you my workin', —
Don't you step on my blue suede shoes,
Hey diddle diddle
I'm playin' my fiddle,
Ain't got nothin' to lose.

Roll over, Beethoven
And tell Tchaikovsky the news.
                        — Roll Over Beethoven

It is not all whimsy & irony, for there is a more personal aspect to Berry's music.[10]

—Yes, oh yes, Long Distance, I'll accept the charge, I'll pay.
Which loved one is calling, I did not hear you say.
Both are deep within my heart, her mom and my Marie.
It's so good to hear your voice from Memphis, Tennessee.

Oh you mean so much to me, more than you'll ever know.
Surely you have not forgot how much I love you so.
If you remember me dear and sometimes talk to me,
Maybe that would re-unite our home in sunny Tennessee.
[. . .]
My heart was torn apart as I looked back at my Marie
And there the pieces still remain with you in Tennessee.
[. . .]
I guess I should stop talking, after all you placed the call.
                        — Little Marie

We imagine, from what we know, what we assume to know, whatever world we do not know.

Berry's version of The Wabash Cannonball, a song supposedly written by A.P. Carter of the original Carter Family, becomes a true hymn to transport, the Negro dream of a cool & righteous escape from his prison of origins:

—Well I left my home in Norfolk, Virginia,
California on my mind,
I straddled that Greyhound
And rode him into Raleigh
And on across to Caroline.
We stopped at Charlotte,
We by-passed Rockhill,
We never was a minute late;

---

[10] Berry's age works to his advantage. A good decade older than the songwriters dealt with in this work, his works reflect the intelligence of an adult, which adds to the sympathetic yet critical content of many of his Teen type songs.

90 miles out of Atlanta by sundown,
Rockin' out of Georgia State.
We had motor trouble
That turned into a struggle
Halfway across Alabam'
And that hound broke down
And left us all stranded
In downtown Birmingham.
Right away I bought me a thru-train ticket
Ridin' across Mississippi, clean
And I was on the Midnight Flyer
Flyin' out of Birmingham,
Smokin' into New Orleans
Somebody helped me to get out of Louisiana
Just to help me get to Houston town.
There are people there who care a little about me
And they won't let a poor boy down.
Sure as you're born
They bought me a silk suit,
They put luggage in my hand
And I woke up high over Albuquerque
On a jet to the Promised Land.

Workin' on a T-bone steak,
I had a party flyin' over the Golden Gate
And the pilot told us in 13 minutes
He would get us at the Terminal gate.
Cut your engines and cool your wings
And let me have it to the telephone.
Los Angeles, give me Norfolk, Virginia,
Tidewater 4-10-0-9,
Tell the folks back home
This is the Promised Land callin'
And the poor boy's on the line.

I saw Chuck Berry for the first time in a movie called *The T.A.M.I. (Teenage American Music International) Show*. It was a fly-by-night closed-circuit TV-style flic that hit the neighborhood movie & vanished a week after it arrived. It was an anthology of currently popular singers & groups; James Brown, Lesley Gore, Gerry & the Pacemakers, Marvin Gaye, the Supremes, Jan & Dean, Smokey Robinson & the Miracles, the Beach Boys, Billy J. Kramer & the Dakotas, the Rolling Stones Etc. It was shot before a trainload of teenagers &

Hollywood-planted teenage extras in the Santa Monica Auditorium.

—*Hey, everybody, see them arrivin',*
  The greatest stars you'll ever see.
  Some are flyin' and some are drivin'
  From Liverpool to Tennessee.
  [. . .]
  Here they come from all over the world,
  A million guitars swingin', dancin' and singin'
  [. . .]
  Don't forget the Motor City sound of the day:
  The baby lovin' Supremes and Marvin Gaye;
  The king of the blues: soulful James Brown;
  The Beach Boys singin' "I Get Around,"
  Yeah, round, round, get around, I get around.
  from *Here They Come (From All Round The World)*
  the theme—song of *The T.A.M.I. Show.*

Jan & Dean open the show sidewalk-surfing thru the closed curtains. Jan grabs ahold of the mike & hollers into it:

—Now! Here he is! The guy who started it all! Chuck! Berry!

Berry ambles down a skeletal staircase, stage-left, playing his low-slung blonde-wood single-cutaway hollow-body Gibson electric guitar. He's wearing a rumpled, white, Panama planter's suit & he's playing Maybelline. As soon as he opens his mouth to sing, a gang of dancing girls dash out in tight skirts, capris, stretch pants, bathing suits, tights, hip-huggers & twist-shimmy dresses. They twist their hips frantically as if to feed them into their cunts, roll their eyes up into a dirty movie, shake their tits, (*O Maybelline, why can't 'cha be true*)
    joined by male dancers dressed in tight pants, T-shirts, sweat-shirts, sneakers, Beatle-boots, chukka boots, who mince, flex & clench their jaws & do the Gene Kelly, dancing around the ladies who dance around themselves as if in orbit. Berry keeps singing, looking dimly amused, detached, while dancers dance before him, behind him & around him.
    Half-way thru his song, you hear the sounds of another group playing Maybelline. Berry's voice fades away as the camera pans into Gerry Marsden's terrifying smile.
    It's Gerry & the Pacemakers! The audience lets loose with an ear-puncturing scream of delight. The quintet from Liverpool is managed by Brian Epstein, the manager of The Beatles. Gerry, the group's lead singer & rhythm guitarist, is a neat little chap, hair combed and parted. He holds his guitar up to his neck & smiles when he sings. His smile is a mechanical invention as regular as the lights on a sign· flashing on & off. The smile reveals bright teeth in a fixed grin. Gerry resembles a ventriloquist's dummy. The Pacemakers &

Gerry sing & smile through more songs.

When they sing Berry's *Nadine* their voices fade into Berry's voice & the camera is back on Chuck Berry, whose wry smile seems to anticipate that end-of-the-night paycheck. He opens his mouth. Bam! male & female dancers come whizzing out before him, while other dancers, isolated on tiered platform (which resemble construction scaffolding & represent the show's only set), go thru assorted contractions & spasms. All the dancers dance different dances all at once. The snake pit Rockettes. Once again Chuck Berry is overwhelmed by dancers.

> (— Berry (is) 38 . . . After serving time for armed robbery and escorting a 14-year-old Apache girl across a state line for "immoral purposes," Berry was recently granted a reprieve by his parole board in St. Louis.
>
> *Time*: May 21, 1965

Gerry & the Pacemakers pick up where Berry left off. Gerry's electronic smile used like a strophe. He often waves his flat-picking hand to Somebody in the audience. Somebody is anybody & the audience screams hysterically whenever he waves at them. No dancers to bother Gerry & the Pacemakers & they sing two more of Chuck Berry's songs.

> (— He is married, with four children, and now lives in Chicago, often spending weekends at his own country club, "Berry Park," in Missouri.
>
> *Rhythm & Blues*: Feb. 1965

The Supremes, a trio of young Negro ladies from Detroit wearing silken 1930/Jean Harlow gowns hanging to their toes, their hair teased into giant bee-hives, sing *Baby Love* & the director decides to apply his art to photographing them. The lead singer, Diana Ross, his principal target.

The camera goes right to her face. Closer & closer. Until her singing profile fills the screen. Closer & closer. Until the lens is nearly into her open mouth. Glimmering saliva, capped teeth dazzling, her neck muscles strain to push out the sound of her shrill voice. The lip line of her mouth is overrun with a clown-like smear of lipstick. She spits out each word as if the taste must be gotten rid of. & the camera stays fixed upon her face & the smile that is constant upon it as she sings. The camera turns her face into a mammoth hate-mask. Her eyes: cold centers of contempt. She looks like a hustler transformed by bitterness & bad mileage by the men whose fear of love destroys love.

—*Ooh, ohh, baby love,*
  My baby love, I need you,
  Oh how I need you!

But all you do is treat me bad,
Break my heart and leave me sad.

Smokey Robinson & the Miracles came on the stage dressed in Cotton Club suits of white. Robinson has the voice of a castrato & his face is like a mulatto Oscar Levant. The Miracles, a vocal trio of middle-aged Negro men cluster around their mike while Smokey unhooks his mike from its stand & holds it in his hand. The mudras of hand-holding a mike are extensive & Smokey attempts a good many of them: including the one where, between lines, he tosses the mike from hand to hand, getting it to his mouth just when the next word is to be sung.

The Miracles harmonize, wave their hands up in the air, wiggle heavily, shuffle painfully, & remind me of the Ink Spots.

All four of them get whipped into a frenzy after the first song. (I had the feeling the frenzy came later in their regular act, but all of the groups were limited to a few numbers.) The hysterical ritual of the frenzy is to sing while dancing &, while dancing, loosen your collar, pull off your tie, throw it to the floor & while dancing & singing & loosening your collar, to take off your jacket & casually throw it onto the floor in the same are demonstrated by a matador executing a good pass; singing, dancing, undressing, doing a split or two: point your fingers somewhere, clench your fists, open your hands, wave, smile, pout, shut your eyes, squeeze them together in the fury of feeling — all of it done, if possible, as if it were incidental & not painstakingly choreographed.

As the applause subsides, the cameras (instead of showing the audience) pan to Smokey & the Miracles bending down to pick up their coats & ties & walk off stage.

Next: Billy J. Kramer & The Dakotas, another English group managed by Epstein ("Billy J. Kramer, perhaps in some ways the best looking pop singer in the world, sent his first two songs to the number one spot and that's not a bad start."[11]) Billy J. has a trimmed d.a. haircut & a weak face. The kind of weak face that looks good to girls when it is 17 & is, in fact, a model of what boys would like to look at 17. But at 21 the face begins to fade into a fat vagueness, the wavy pompadour gets waxy, the mouth gets drawn & the chin loses its point merging into twin chin, & the eyes, those bright brown jewels beneath sexy half-shut lids, become like rat-eyes.

Billy J. is built like the 1940 crooner. In fact he looks like Johnny Desmond. They both tilted their heads to one side, slacked the tension in their lower lip & sang out of the side of their mouth.

Billy J., like Gerry Marsden, winks & waves at the audience while he sings. 3rd rate: a local singer on a local talent show that loses out to a local basketball star who does impersonations.

Then James Brown & the Famous Flames, a Negro group, comes on. & on.

---

[11]Epstein. *Cellarful of noise.* Doubleday. 1964.

Brown's a small man solidly put together. A huge construction of hair: a glistening, curly tower atop his skull: adds at least 2 inches to his height. Black & white checkered vest & jacket, black pants, black silk shirt & a white tie. The ex-shoeshine boy from Augusta, Georgia, has a huge head on his short body & he sings in a high voice that is a scream, a whistle, a red-alert (Konelrad) & a prophecy.

The Famous Flames are a quartet who sing with Brown &, like the Miracles, indulge in a lot of gesturing, sudden physical eruptions, flailing, flamboyant stances, dances & good-natured mugging.

Pure Dynamite! KING LP 883:

Not having had a good night's sleep for 3 days, I walked home from work in a fatigue-trance. Partying, drinking with friends, writing in honor of dawn & having to wake up after not having gone to sleep in order to go to work. See the Zombie: my new dance, a stone-age shuffle clomp.

I shuffled into a record store having its weekly Going Out Of Business Sale / This is IT! & bought the James Brown album *Pure Dynamite!* Tina was crazy about *Oh Baby Don't You Weep* which was a cut on the album.

—*Oh, baby, don't you weep.*
  Doo doop doop dee doop.
  I want you to play a little softer now.

James Brown on the stage in a gold lame suit sparkling in the spotlight, his mouth open wide with song on the album cover.

I took the bus home & fell asleep twice before my stop.

We ate dinner, got the kids to bed, then put the new record on the player.

Before anything: sounds of the audience screaming. The bash of a drum. A brass section explodes with instant brass blats & bleats & bleats & — *It's THE JAMES! BROWN! SHOW!!!* screams the M.C. over the lion's-den growl of the audience.

In our sleep-hunger the rest of the record is like listening to a Hitler Youth meeting.

Say, ma-an: Where didchya get them shoes, ma-a-nn?
(The audience grumbles & moans because somebody on stage is trying to bug James Brown.)
At the shoe-store, answers Brown.
(The audience screams with delight & approval. The rhythm section is working behind Brown.)
You sure is clean!
(The audience cheers. It's like the audience I was a member of when I was a kid & went to Saturday morning movie serials. *YA*YYY*YYY!!!!*)

Brown uses his voices. Some sound as if sung *in extremis*; others reach stein-breaking intensity. He gasps & whispers in decibels louder than a screaming man impaled beneath a tractor. & the audience, gasping, hollering, swooning, yelling — & you can hear them hearing him, responding to his song in a submissive trance of worship. It is like I imagine the audience must have been when Hitler was before them, or FDR, — how they love the image before them because it frees them of the image before the mirror, before the militias.

Yeah, yeah! You SURE is clean!

This life, it's a dream, this worshipping of those who stand before us on stages; a dream of a zone beyond sleep: an ideal to keep us going; entertainment to hush despair, the lost quest, the unheeded call.

Tina leaves the living room to get ready for bed.
The big James Brown band, a ceremonial brass group making sounds of the blown *shofar*. The drums rumble Babel's foundation. James Brown turns his voice into a police-whistle, into the sound of a nerve pulled out of his loins still spitting its final electrical pulse.)

Brown & the Famous Flames bound onto the *T.A.M.I. Show*'s stage like track-stars & don't stop the race until the race is run. They put on a show in a tradition of show-giving I was exposed to as a kid: the 10 act vaudeville show. The whole works — magic, acrobats, comedians, dancers.
Brown sings a song with a full comprehension of the Book of Gestures: all the *mudras & bandhas* essential to the movement of his body & the motion of song. Tie loosened, coat thrown to the floor (retrieved by one of the Famous Flames who keeps singing as he stoops to pick it up). Gangster Cagney stances. Sweat forms early beneath the rise of his teased turret of glistening curls. The cameras close-up to his face to follow song's agony: sweat, muscled neck wide with the efforts of expelling song. Sometimes he moves like a boxer pushing off his opponent, or stalking him, backing him against the ropes

—I think it was back in 1959,
 He said, Darlin', you send me.
 He said to call me.
 I'll come runnin' back to you.

Then Brown sings his first big hit (1956) *Please, Please, Please*

—Please, please, please, please, please don't go!
 Please, please, please, don't go, honey.

114

He falls to his knees holding the mike in his hands like a lover & wails without restraint in time with the beat. One of the Famous Flames (Bobby Byrd), who earlier picked up Brown's discarded sports coat, picks Brown off the floor, takes the mike out of Brown hand, sets it a right, then leads him tenderly off stage, draping Brown's checkered sports coat around heaving shoulders. Brown looks ahead, fierce tragedy in his eyes.

Suddenly Brown snaps around, rushes back to the mike, grabs it like an old-time movie-star grabbing a fluttery heroine & bending her back to kiss her. He falls to his knees & begins screaming & sobbing, louder than before.

—*Baby, you've done me wrong,*
  Took my love and now you're gone
  Baby, take my hand.
  Please, please, please, please, please don't go!

Again he is picked up off the floor by Bobby Byrd & led off-stage: Byrd's face & bearing revealing brotherly sympathy & compassion

PLEASE! PLEASE! PLEASE! PLEASE! PLEASE!

Brown's eyes shut tight to scream a shriek unlike anything within ken: a sound of madness, release, horror & triumph — a scream to greet the end of civilization with.

He ends the act rushing back on stage to do a frantic rubber leg dance. Several splits, arching back further with each split until you are afraid that he might tear in half —

—Here, take this part, that part. (Gods disassemble themselves for the devout so the devout can touch that part of a god worshipped above other parts.)

—Here, take my fabled 9 foot prick & tyre your trucks with it; here, take my fabled soul, set it into space, & build a new world upon the new planet

No one publicly devours the flesh of the gods they privately cannibalize but at odd hours, day & night, you might hear teeth munching into flesh & bone of gods —

•

—*Here we come again,*
  Catch us if you can.
  Time to get a move on.
  We will yell with all our might:
  Catch us if you can,
  Catch us if you can,
  Catch us if you can,
  Catch us if you can.
            #3 / *Catch Us If You Can*: The Dave Clark 5

Current Myths:

The Defense Dept. has invented a device that releases a sound ray to explode the eye-ball;

Y'know it doesn't make any difference. The death you face is final, friend. No more woundings; just killings.

We fight the Orient so many times. The East whose lesson is finally that wisdom is not enough. Wisdom is, as wisdom always was, the man who is wise.

—Who is the coolest guy who is what am?
  Fast talkin', slow walkin', good lookin' Mohair Sam.
    #11 / *Mohair Sam*: Charlie Rich

UNKNOWNS, BOUNTYS, LEON THE LEISURES, INMATES, MARVELS, DAVE & THE CUSTOMS, CAPT. BEEFHEART, LIMEY & THE YANKS, PIRANNAS, BEETHOVENS, PRIMADONS, CHADILLACS, ALDERMEN, SECRETS, GRANDEURS; L.A. MYSTICS, OUTSIDERS, GALAXIES, BLACK & BLUES, AH! THOSE ROGUES, YA YA WHISKS;

BERKELEY, high quality amplifier incorporating variable length reverberation and multi-speed variable depth vibrato. Two inputs, separate tone and volume controls. Amplifier and loudspeaker units in separate cabinets to give greater power without feedback.

$750.00

SUPER BEATLE: This is the choice of the world famous Beatles and many other famous groups. Recognized around the world for its 200 watt power output and unrivaled for its sheer, undistorted power.

$1500.00

INTRUDERS, MYSTERIES, NOMADS, FIREBALLS, JACK & THE TREMBLERS, TERRY & THE PIRATES, PSY-KICKS

Chet Atkins 17" Electrotone hollow body with simulated "F" holes • Filter 'Tron bridge pickup and new Super 'Tron II (Jazz) fingerboard pickup • Standby switch • Padded back • Gold-plated Gretsch Bigsby Tremolo and Tailpiece • Built-in double muffler.

$575.00

MODEL 602 / PEDAL CONTROL VOLUME
Handsome lightweight aluminum
base and treadle. Nylon racks
and gear action (no cords or
springs). Rubber treads. De-
tachable cable. List $32.50

FIRST EVER INVENTED!　　FIRST WITH MUSICIANS!
BOBBY LEE ORIGINAL NO-MISHAP GUITAR STRAP!
BOBBY LEE 3 in 1 PICK: Single string or Unison Effect or Rhythm
　　　　　　　• More Pick-up Power
　　　　　　　• Balance your Magnetic Field
　　　　　　　Available bright lustre chrome with black insert
　　　　　　　— or bright gold with white insert
　　　　　　　List $25.50

—I say step to the left now
　Step to the right now
　Do the Boomerang now
　Say, do all a-them things, girl
　I say now!
　Yep, yep, yep, yep.
　Yep.yep,yep,yep,yep,yep.
　Now, what I say?
　I said, now,
　Yep, yep, yep, yep.
　Yep, yep, yep.
　Now what I say?
　　　　　　　Do The Boomerang: Jr. Walker

•

NASHVILLE / THE SOUTH of fundamentalist religions to ease the base white terror of
blackness; of two-headed coins that you flip in order to, 1st flip, speak of Mother in rhetoric
of worship & awe & then, 2nd flip, go out & gangbang a 17 year old high school student
beyond repair;
　　honkeytonks & juke joints; the south of Robert Frank, Walker Evans, Dorothea Lange,
F.S.A. (Farm Security Administration) photographs of rutted depression land & weathered
faces facing the cameras that look as ruined as the land they can no longer use;
　　of wood-slat, tin cup, cardboard window panes — pain so intense there is no name for
it & all a man can do is chew wood or smash his fist against a fence post until the fist is soft
& useless as the earth beneath him that he falls to & sleeps on — dreams do not allow him
to forget what he cannot name;
　　Greyhound South: 9 for $1 hamburger shanties, Quonset-hut movie theaters, Dr.
Pepper, screen doors, flypaper, shotguns

—Well, they said you was high-classed,
　Well, that was just a lie.

117

Well, you ain't never caught a rabbit
And you ain't no friend of mine.
                    Hound Dog: Elvis

   The South whose jungles hold in their dark green unknown mutant animals who have
no eyes nor cars & whose appendages are spiked & thorned;
   a broken South still unbent, maintaining its monarchies, kingdoms, hierarchies, with a
fanaticism essential to the winning of wars.
   A revealed violence in his sensual mouth, shirt open, dancing on his toes; then back
onto the balls of his feet, weaving in & out.

—Rhythm is somethin' you have or don't have, but when you have it, you have it all over.

—I—I really can't seem to help moving, and I don't really — really I don't — mean to offend
people. Y'see, my mother taught me to believe in God, and when I was just a little boy,
she took me to the Pentecostal Holiness Church where the emotions out of love of God
naturally led to body movements.

   Elvis was wild & tame, life & fortune tamed him. He is unmarried surrounds himself
with a group of friends & colleagues from Nashville who keep Elvis amused: Presley doesn't
smoke or drink & all reporters who interview him say that he's polite, courteous & totally
impersonal. He owns two homes, one in Nashville, the other in Hollywood. Both are
furnished with pinball machines, jukeboxes, soft-drink bars, TVs, stuffed animals, books,
toys — & he plays touch-football with his buddies or they'll sing together & goof-off within
the fenced, policed land of his two homes.

—*You just a natural born beehive*
  Filled with honey to the top,
  But I ain't greedy, baby,
  All I want is all you got.
                    A Big Hunk Of Love: Elvis

   Elvis is in fame's prison & he is a docile willing prisoner. Kept amused by his friends
who are, in most ways, no different than he; he is served by his facsimiles. His revolt was a
success. His wild earth-dance is over. His imitators & followers are rarely heard today.
   The revolt's done when the revolutionary force becomes an established institution,
itself a target for a future revolution. Today Presley is a blank paper for the imagination's
marker to work on. The animal god, violent prince, the adolescent's ideal sex image, has
been trapped & lives content in captivity.

"Speaking of the American flag, (Presley) automatically and without trace of embarrassment holds up his right hand as though taking an oath to honor it"

Photoplay: June/65

—*Every sinner looks for something*
That will put his heart at ease.
There is only one true answer,
He must get down on his knees.
Meet your neighbor in the chapel
Join with him in tears of joy

Crying In The Chapel: Elvis

"The boys spent two-and-a-half hours visiting Elvis Presley and manager Colonel Parker. For a couple of hours they joined Elvis in a rock session on the car load of guitars provided by the Colonel. Ever candid, Paul (McCartney) told Elvis bluntly that he preferred the Tupelo lad's style in Elvis' early days when it was 'wild.'"

K.Y.A, Beat: Sept. 25/65

—*Oh, yeh, I'll tell you something*
I think you'll understand.
Then I'll say that something,
I want to hold your hand,
I want to hold your hand,
I want to hold your hand.

Oh please say to me
And let me be you man
And please say to me
You'll let me hold your hand,
Now, let me hold your hand,
I want to hold your hand.

I Want To Hold Your Hand: The Beatles

was the first Beatles song I heard & then I couldn't say anything about it because they hadn't entered my realm of culture. There was a whispering about the Beatles, every so often their faces on a magazine cover. An odd looking quartet;

John Lennon, mite-mouthed, somewhat like George Sanders;

George Harrison, out of *Oliver Twist*, with his eyebrows growing into each other — a bucket of uncombed long hair around his skull;

Paul McCartney, doe-eyed, starlet-nosed, bow-lipped;

& finally Ringo Starr with big ears, thick nose, full mouth, a cabbage patch of hair, whose gentle homeliness gives him a tragic character which the faces of his partners lack.

YOU'RE THE GEAR
. . . What the Beatles think of Beatle people — fab, smashing, super, screamie

I still couldn't understand who they were or why they were what they were. The jukebox in the neighborhood bar had Beatles records. It never had anything but jazz before.

—*Well, she was just seventeen,*
You know what I mean,
And the way she looked was way beyond compare.
So how could I dance with another,
Oh, when I saw her standing there.
> *I Saw Her Standing There*: The Beatles

The kids of a dear friend, a musician, were crazy about the Beatles. The youngest, a boy, 4 years old, could sing all the Beatles songs. The oldest girl, 10 years old, wept herself to sleep for two nights in a row after seeing the Beatles' first movies, *A Hard Day's Night*.

One of my wife's closest friends told us about the movie with such rapture and reverence that we were, despite earlier hesitation, eager to see it. A folk-singer we knew at that time (who is now a member of a highly successful rock & roll group) went into a rapturous trance before a jukebox playing *I Want To Hold Your Hand* —he looked, as he raised his head up, like a man whose prayer had just been answered by God.

I heard a band of children on a hilltop chanting
Yeah! yeah! yeah! yeah!
Yeah! yeah yeah!

The newborn, unknown, child-gods strike the soul of children, orphans & men who grow old with a stiffness in their hearts.

Then, Beatles were everywhere. On the covers of *Life* & *The Saturday Evening Post*; paperback books about them on the newsstands; magazines from England about the Beatles & also about other groups like the Beatles; pins, pillows; dolls; bubblegum — but I was not persuaded. The sounds of their music would reach my communications-center every so often & I thought it was pretty poor. Loud, often off-key, & sloppy.

—*She loves you. yeh, yeh, yeh,*
She loves you, yeh, yeh, yeh,
She loves you, yeh, yeh, yeh, yeh.
> *She Loves You*: The Beatles

What is fame is when a man decides, regarding fame, that fame has escaped him. It is a nostalgia for what a man is not, a grief that leads to worship.

The Beatles are the revolution. There can be no doubt of it. They are unavoidable. Their faces & their music surrounds us. They inspire & direct an entirely new culture filled with people who impersonate various ritual steps the Beatles took in their ascent to greatness. Within the design of our time & culture, the Beatles maintain their evolution & continue developing their talents. Though the culture is overcrowded with synthetic Beatles, no one has ever been able to sound like them.

—*Ah-oo, ah-oo,*
You've been good to me,
You made me glad when I was blue
And eternally I'll always be in love with you
And all I gotta do, is
Thank you girl.
Thank You Girl: The Beatles

All four have been dedicated to the gods of popular music since their early teens. Their gods were performers like Eddie Cochran, Lonnie Donnegan, Carl Perkins, Bill Haley & the Comets, Little Richard, the Everly Brothers, Chet Atkins, Muddy Waters, Bo Diddley — &, of course. Elvis Presley.

Never leave the fetish-house upright. Death is resurrection.

Ringo was constantly ill as a child (appendicitis, peritonitis, broken pelvic fibers from falling out of a hospital bed, 14 operations) & got his first set of drums when he was 13. Paul was plagued with mystery rashes. His first instrument was a banjo which he got when he was 11. His mother died when he was 14. George was a sickly child bothered by an annual spell of laryngitis that desisted when he was 13. He got his first guitar when he was 14. John's mother died when he was 14. It was she who taught him to play the banjo when he was 12.

They were all born during WWII in Liverpool a northern industrial seaport city in England; a gritty, tough lower middle-class city cluttered with congested dwellings, grimy pubs & clubs. After many attempts & many group combinations (John & Paul together did an act billed as The Nurk Twins; other groups they formed were The Quarrymen, Moondogs, The Silver Beatles) the group found its momentum.

After the death of an original member & the mysterious dismissal of their regular drummer (because "George Martin (a record producer at E.M.l.) had not been too happy about Pete Best's drumming, and the Beatles . . . decided his beat was wrong for their music"[12]) the Beatles began their ascension.

"Many people ask what are Beatles? Why Beatles? Ugh, Beatles? How did the name arrive?

---

[12] Epstein. *Cellarful of noise*. Doubleday. 1964.

So we will tell you. It came in a vision — a man appeared on a flaming pie and said unto them, 'From this day on you are Beatles with an *A*.' Thank you Mister Man, they said, thanking him." Writes John Lennon on the genesis of their name.

In true shamanic tradition, they were initiated in a cave, learning their basic magical functions. The Beatles' basic training was performing in the Cavern[13], a cellar club in Liverpool, where they began to cultivate a fanatical following of teenage females. (It is essential to know that the fans of popular singers are primarily female. There is a Beatle-legend told of a concert in Paris where the audience was 80% male because the French fan is primarily male. It threw the Beatles off because they were used to performing before screaming girls, whereas the French male fan listened quietly to the music.) As gods, their history is the history of how they birthed the god in themselves; how they served the mysteries integral within their instinctive vision, their dream of fame.

"Aion is a child playing dice and jesting; the kingdom is the child's."
                    Heraclitus

—Another point requires our attention: the songs. According to ancient testimonies, songs played a great part in the mysteries. Palmphos and Musaeus were believed to have composed songs which the Lycomedes used to sing during the enactment of the mysteries. All the prophets of Orphism, beginning with Orpheus himself, were believed to have been excellent singers. Iamblichus alludes to songs which prepared the neophytes for the epiphany of the gods . . . Symbols, images and songs all point to a single aim: excite the imagination of the initiates and produce visions in accordance with certain dogmas and belief.[14]
           from: *From Orpheus to Paul*, Macchioro

None of them really sing well, especially Ringo who has hard time keeping key, surrendering early in a song — but the ear responds to their intent; the ear bends to consider the concept of their music. It is their Sound — a scared word that record-producers whisper of in cathedral tones & their agents cluck of — their sound: a grail, a mythic needle to tattoo a race with.

—*Baby's good to me,*
  You know she's happy as can be,
  You know she said so.

---

[13] For proper mythic content you could equate The Cavern to a womb: a symbolic womb, a cosmic egg.

[14] Macchioro, Vittorio. From Orpheus to Paul: a History of Orphism. NY: Holt, 1930

I'm in love with her and I feel fine.
I Feel Fine: The Beatles

McCartney & Lennon write most of the songs the Beatles sing. Lennon writes the words (& sometimes writes the music too). The words are uniformly uninteresting; at times they are barely articulate. The words are not meant to be heard as words. They are sounds within the sound the Beatles make. Almost all of the songs are love songs & are replete with the clichés of pop-music romanticism: a mashed-potato rhetoric of repeated words.[15]

—It's true, yes it is,
I could be happy with you by my side
If I could forget her,
But it's my pride, yes it is, yes it is,
Oh, yes it is true,
Yes it is, it's true, yes it is, it's true.
                    Yes It Is: The Beatles

They are the angels of white light as they re-arrange gravity to demonstrate the Star's traditional grace & to show the distance of immortals who move in a different round than we. We have chosen them to combat darkness for us, to uphold the illusion of whiteness.

Q. Are you as lazy as they say?
A. Not at all, replied George Harrison. I'm quite active. When I was born in 1943 I was twenty inches long. Look at me now.

They are irreverent in a way that makes them innocent of the world's dark implications. They are Alexander before the Gordian knot; — the travelling players of the commedia dell'arte: they are Pantalone, Pulcinella, Coviello, Harlequin; — they are 4 men from Megara singing the song of the komos; — they stay in the lightning's center & the illumination from that ring is the energy of maya.

—Help! I need somebody!
Help! Not just anybody.
Help! You know I need someone.
Help!
                    Help: The Beatles

---

[15] Their most recent album, Rubber Soul, contains a few songs (Norwegian Wood, In My Life, What Goes On, Girl, & Run For Your Life) show a growing concern with word-content.

Popular culture is a brave empire though its foundations are most frail. It attempts to combat (or conceal) the dark core of earth tangled in the hearts of men, while the unpopular culture has become a factory constructed to reduce the darkness into popular culture.

JOHN: You can analyze anything — what someone thinks of a bottle of milk, if you like — if you believe in that stuff. You can go on and on analyzing, creating theories and philosophies about them — but in the end it doesn't really mean anything and it doesn't matter anyway.

HONORARIUMS:
Recently Queen Elizabeth gave out her annual awards called "The Order of the British Empire" and the Beatles were among the recipients.[16]

Civil rights groups are arguing over ABC TV's new Beatle animated cartoon series debuting this fall. Objections are being voiced on the ground that the series is being produced partly in Australia, which has an immigration policy that bar non-whites.[17]

The 1966-67 edition of "Who's Who in America" will contain biographies of the Beatles. . . (the publisher states his reasons as follows) "The verve, freshness, and rollicksome humor of their music and antics are refreshingly creative as well as commercially advantageous.[18]

John has another wild book on sale called "Spaniard In The Works" . . . George is turning out self-penned for future record release . . . and inventing a "Harrison guitar" which he hopes to produce and get on the market . . . they will probably be recording for their own production company when their E.M.I. contract expires.[19]

Dignity, nobility
Our gods are above us, in plain view, to remind us of ascension's principles.
Flying overhead, what if they were to turd-bomb us?
Had Peter Pan ever considered that?

—*We love you Beatles,*
 Yes we do.
 We love you Beatles
 And we'll be true.
 When you're not near us we're blue.

---

[16] *Beatles #6: Summer, 1965* Also contains an article, *How The Beatles Changed My Life*, by 14 yr old Holly Stevens wherein she describes how being a Beatle fan helped her to 1) lose the blues 2) lose weight 3) make friends 4) listen to jazz & Andres Segovia because George does &, finally, 5) increased her knowledge of world affairs: — "Every night I'd look through the papers to see what was new in the Beatles' world. I'd find something, and often, other articles would catch my eye . . . after a time, I seemed to know more about what was going on in the world.
[17] Ibid.
[18] Ibid.
[19] Ibid.

Oh, Beatles, we love you,
Yeah, yeah, yeah!
                    We Love You Beatles: The Carefrees

Each time we are destroyed, we are renewed. We attempt to find our center & to locate the Center of the World. As a shaman drummer re-evaluates the world through his séance & within his trance, so do those gathered before him. They attempt to approach themselves by losing themselves. It is a healing process. The shaman who heals had to die, speak with the gods, in order to return as healer.

—*Can't buy me love, love,*
 Can't buy me love.
 I'll buy you a diamond ring, my friend,
 If it makes you feel alright,
 I'll get you anything, my friend,
 For I don't care too much for money,
 For money can't buy me love
                    Can't Buy Me Love: The Beatles

The creative capitalist is one who makes us forget that we are supporting him.

Like all gods, the Beatles sing for their supper. They're in it for the money. Wealth is the ultimate in contemporary Western hagiology. Our myths never tire substantiating Success by using that Geiger-counter that measures Cash.

The story of gods is also the story of divine capitalism. Religion is the history of corporations. According to its gospel, we must earn whatever we want — whatever we need must be, one way or the other, paid for.

Men support their habits. Only during moments of revolt or creation is man not addicted, or habit-bound. Yet successful revolt lays the ground for new habits, a network of new obligations — new dues paid-out to the same old union.

The revolution is over as soon as your face is printed on sweat shirts worn by the young.

"The Beatles' manager, Brian Epstein, has been working diligently for more than a year trying to get an insurance policy to protect his investment and future should anything fatal happen to the rock 'n' rollers. He finally succeeded in getting the policy with Lloyd's of London the other day and is now beneficiary of a $15 million insurance setup!"
        S.F. Chronicle: Sun. July 25/65

—"Hello, my name is Jill."
—"Do we know each other?" I asked her.
—"Yes we do. I love you and you love me. We shall have to marry." I was certain I had never seen her before.

—"Who introduced us and when?" I asked.

—"It was God himself who did it," she replied, and added, — "If you don't love me now, can't you at least try to learn to love me?"

A story told by Paul McCartney

"In London, Beatle John Lennon got a mild shock when his father, Freddie, went into competition against him. The elder Lennon, a 53-year-old erstwhile seaman and dishwasher, signed up as a performer with Britain's Pye Records and cut a disc featuring a monologue of personal reminiscence called 'That's My Life,' and, on the flip, a song entitled 'The Next Time You Feel Important.' 'It would be kind of nice,' said Papa Lennon, 'to knock the Beatles off the top of the pops.'"

Newsweek: December 20, 1965

—"You never asked after Fred Lennon," he said, disappointed. (Fred is his father; he emerged after they got famous.) "He was here a few weeks ago. It was only the second time in my life I'd seen him — I showed him to the door." He went on cheerfully: "I wasn't having him in the house."

Interview with John Lennon

O the kids! the kids!
the kids put down old people for war bombs doom-buttons booby traps reactionary death rotten bodies false values corrupting menace misunderstanding total loneliness actual lack of contact lack of touch & adult compassion;

O the kids form bandit packs & raid & sack our cities; defile the churches, schools, shrines & palaces; overthrow buses & mutilate gardens & deface museum walls;

O the kids, the kids, would fight each other to death for the chance to dismember a Beatle in the ritual name of love;

Who are the kids who loiter like fire-hydrants in front of malt shops, drive-ins, back lots, alley ways, street corners, hamburger stands — who drive down Broadway looking for a whore who will give them everything they want without questioning pimples, rudeness, embarrassment;

"Mythology, like the severed head of Orpheus, goes on singing even in death and from afar. In its lifetime, among the peoples where it was indigenous, it was not only sung like a kind of music, it was also lived. Material though it was, for those peoples, its carrier, it was a form of expression, thought, and life."

from: *Essays On A Science Of Mythology* by C. Kercnyi

Who are they, the young, who slink & creep down street with bland looks of sage or cretin or worn-out students of Huysmans 50 years of degeneracy on their milky pimply skin wearing bulky romantic welder jackets boots wraparound sunglasses skin-grabbing pants;

who released from home or school giggle down alleyways passing on fables of commerce based on collective standards of haberdashery & transportation, wheels, & chicks who, as the story goes, go for them & only them in the backseat of cars or in movie-house balconies or behind penal bushes sniped at by binoculars & degenerate policemen;

who opens the door to the street, bombed-out, with a smile; wiped-out on premature pot or pilfered pills from nervous mother of sometimes-father, the sunshine crashing down upon him;

who are they the always new loudly proclaiming unsureness?

—The target reveals the hunter's fear;

Who are they

the In Crowd the Pepsi Generation the Mods the Rockers the Beat Scene (name into name into name) maintaining their path talking about sport heroes & candy bars & transistor radios & votive 45 rpm sacrament to pile upon the phallic spindle & for hours listen to the music, sexual fairytales, gather up dream strength to go out & insult your beloved when she walks by in her girl pack (shining in sunlight in vinyl coats white Corrèges vinyl boots);

who worship underground roots of blackness in a worn white heart; the fix of darkness

Who are the kids who kill in their dreams & pee in their pants when hit in actual, accidental combat; — whose kid is it that love another male by beating him senseless for a reason neither know; puking up contraband beer into the lap of his over-made-up, under-age, pick-up;

Who are the kids whose days & hearts are filled with the glory of words & sights & sounds & whose nights are terrorized by screaming parents, knife clattering to the floor, broken window, lamp knocked down, blackness, sirens;

Whose kids are they who can't ask questions? Whose kids are they who keep answering back, yackety-yak, (O Mother O Father O Tired Out God) Whose kids are those kids who commit unspeakable tribal crimes & in the newspaper photograph of them look so neat & decent;

bopping down the street. Bam bam bam. Bangs his fist into his hand. Bam bam bam. Cracks his knuckles, spits as much as he can. His breath a fog of old cigarette smoke. He is a follower of religious order, that's who he is. A novitiate in the sacred youth —small cult of Fame whose sacred figures are hermaphroditic reincarnations who sing about possible & impossible love & protest racial discrimination, atomic bombs & loneliness on brilliant TV screen surrounded by big breasted Hollywood (Babylonian/Cretian) women & muscled men on stages where Rome is remembered the pits the dens the lions in movies. *Quo Vadis?* in home movies of Hiroshima maidens in newsreels newspapers in magazines in comic books wherever the eye alerts to roost, they are there —the Gods of Fame

HOLLYWOOD —   GLAMOUR   —   LIGHTS

EXCITEMENT

The SPOTLIGHT ON *YOU!*

BE A FAMOUS RECORDING STAR!

in a frenzy to submit to the new world order we form our bands, spend fortunes on electronic equipment, grow male hair until it furls into female locks & commence singing

commence wiggling
commence our totem-waving fantasy
saying Hello;

rewarded by Time because they are time's servants because they are timely they must be tracked like a space-capsule beep on the radar screen in the darkness of our minds our heart beep beep in James Bond's eyes glowering in his cell invincible Mike Hammer's pilgrim progress blood marks on the brick walls Dick Tracy Batman Tarzan Mr. Clean in darkness they are but the hide of the huge Uroboros they fester on for transit into timelessness
deep into the primordial

elemental disaster of Eden

What value? what ethic? what to guide a man from one wilderness (that of his youth) into another wilderness

"in her purse she carries a lipstick that contains a deadly poison gas, a comb that turns into a sharp dagger, a cigarette lighter which is actually a portable flamethrower. Her false fingernails are very sharp steel blades. Her name is 'Modesty Blaise' . . . another movie called The Tenth Victim . . . where the film's props include exploding bananas, bullet shooting cameras, electronic weapons and Ursula Andress. Her arsenal includes a 'sex shooter'— a metallic rapid fire brassiere. In one scene she fires her 'bang-bang' bra by expanding her chest, kills an Oriental assailant, and blows away the smoke coming out of the two breast muzzles . . . 'The Tenth Victim' also strives to be morally instructive."
SF Sunday Examiner & Chronicle: Sept 26 / 1965

is love as large as the myth of it? Is it real? Why is something real, what makes it so? (spools of disorder reeling off words, rattling out un-filled data — *the universe needs processing*!) what is to be found? can we ever really understand each other or know each other — we who cannot touch the reality of our gods cannot touch the reality of ourselves.

What is death? Am I alive?

What is success, what is failure, who are heroes, what are gods?

Ghosts of illusions live in my mind. They multiply like mice. Ah you should hear the population explosion inside the ivory nut shell! (I scheme to propose primers of power & primers of failure be written & used as textbooks in our high schools.) But I drift, — to the musics. I offer this guide by Ezra Pound:

"When you start searching for 'pure elements' in literature you will find that literature has been created by the following· classes of persons:
1. Inventors. Men who found a new process, or whose extant work gives us the first known example of a process.
2. The masters. Men who combined a number of such processes, and who used them as well as or better than the inventors.

3. The diluters. Men who came after the first two kinds of writer, and couldn't do the job quite as well.

4. Good writers without salient qualities. Men who are fortunate enough to be born when the literature of a given country is in good working order, or when some particular branch of writing is 'healthy'. For example, men who wrote sonnets in Dante's time, men who wrote short lyrics in Shakespeare's time, or for several decades thereafter, or who wrote French novels and stories after Flaubert had shown them how.

5. Writers of belles-lettres. That is, men who didn't really invent anything, but who specialized in some particular part of writing, who couldn't be considered as 'great men' or as authors who were trying to give a complete presentation of life, or of their epoch.

6. The starter of crazes."

from: *A.B.C. OF READING*: New Directions, NY, n.d..

•

Texas turned me on to Bob Dylan. My friend Larry McMurtry, the novelist, wrote about hearing Dylan's first album: You've got to hear him. He's the best white blues singer you'll ever hear today.

I bought the album[20], read the liner notes by Nat Hentoff, put the record on the player & was truly delighted with Dylan's offering. A 20 year old kid with a voice that was voices: a Lon Chaney with Rimbaud's face. A Hassidic gangster Dead End kid. Puffing on a mouth harp, flat-picking his D-28, his version of Roy Acuff's *Freight Train Blues* was a joyful event, as was so much of that 1st album (*House of The Rising Sun, In My Time Of Dyin', Baby Let Me Follow You Down, Fixin' To Die*). His own songs on the album failed to impress me.

Dylan was young in a way that makes a person consider what was right or wrong about his own youth. A tough kid with lean shanks & the innocent hero's heart whose soul contains all the ancient terror. Soon his face wore the drawn gaunt look of faces of youths liberated from WWII's concentration camps.

Newsweek discovered that he was Bob Zimmerman, the eldest son of Abe Zimmerman, an appliance dealer in Hibbing, Minnesota. Bob Zimmerman changed his name to Bob Dylan, it is said, in honor of the Welsh bard Dylan Thomas. (Thomas died overwhelmed with excess, success, rage & furious wounds, a God-haunted anguish. His was a public dying flamboyant & tragic; an assault against the order. Bards disturb the peace by dying in doorways & attracting flies almost immediately. Like Brendan Behan's public dying or Fitzgerald or Hemingway or Hank Williams. Their deaths haunt mourners with a sense of incompletion that becomes a nostalgia, the after-death torment the living indulge in — what-could-have-happened-if . . .) His first mentor (guru) was Woody Guthrie,[21] the

---

[20] *Bob Dylan*: Columbia: CL 1779

[21] Guthrie's book, *Bound For Glory*, is a memorable work.

Oklahoma poet & singer. Dylan made a zealot's pilgrimage to the east to commune with Guthrie, who had been ailing for many years with Huntington's chorea, an incurable nervous disorder. The legend does not detail the encounter. The aftermath of it was that Dylan was on his own, without a guru.

The next album,[22] as all that followed, contained only material by Dylan. The songs that were good were true & honestly stated. The songs were more than what had ever been sung to a young generation of consumers. To a young generation, his songs provided the map of a romantic dream, a poetry made out of fierce adolescent wit, an attack on the traditional institutions, never heard before.

The albums started appearing more frequently & on each album cover there was a new face: 6 albums, 6 different faces. His work, like that of Rimbaud, is a masterpiece of youth. Shaking the tree, pointing his finger to the madness in the center of a spiritless world, Dylan can offer no solution. He can only be an example for the tribe, a profound & uneasy reminder that youth is the conscience of our world.

The news Dylan brings to us is the news of himself. Today his hair is long & wild, gone are the surplus khaki pants & work-shirts he wore when he was extending the tradition left by Woody Guthrie. Today he plays an electric guitar & is backed up by a rock 'n' roll band. Dylan is a Beatle at this moment, though the lyric content of his songs surpasses that of any popular songs written today. He is still growing & his growth breeds an envy & fear among his peers. His songs are becoming more wordy, more literary, & repetitively pessimistic. They offer an arctic rage & puzzled hollering. His records are selling much better than ever before. Success is the reward for his glorious fuck you to the steam-roller

Success is the necessary protection our culture surrounds its darkest heart with. It is, at once, a challenge & the challenge's trophy; it is, at once, target & mirror; it is hungered for & it is an inducement to starve; it is, at once, yielded to the challenger & withheld from him until he yields to it; fame is, at once, too easy to obtain & then too hard to relinquish; like power, success is served & can possess its owner until its owner loses his own power in its service.

Dylan's uniqueness becomes the model for his generation to serve. When you commit a revolt that works, you often find that you are in competition with yourself. Every corner you turn you might bump into yourself. What is unique becomes commonplace. What is your talent becomes the echo of it. In this way revolt is destroyed by allowing it to occur, embracing it, packaging it, feeding it to those who crave it, or making hungry those who do not crave it.

"Dylan was a mess — he struts around like a rooster and slops away on stage bashing his electric guitar while mumbling unintelligible words into the mike — backed by a mediocre

---

[22] *The Freewheelin' Bob Dylan*: Columbia: CL 1986

band which was only saved partially by the drummer . . . Dylan was booed and finally had to come on with his regular guitar and do some of his old standards— this is of course what often happens to pop singers when they want to change their style or approach their audience won't like it!"

> from: "Key To The Highway" / Chris Strachwitz, *Rag Baby* 1:3, Berkeley, 1965

The disguises are most evident in the beginnings when a man has enthusiasm but little knowledge to support it. Dylan's evolution, his pilgrim's progress, has been spent in finding the right face: a formal quest to create himself thru his art. In 5 years Dylan has evolved from a cherub-faced folksinger of great promise into the symbolic spokesman of the intelligent young. His protesting has turned more towards the expression of his own immediate experience, his particular condition. For it becomes harder to be responsible towards large pronouncements unless you have answers & solutions. As most popular culture gods, Dylan brings us no law.[23]

His love songs, as a rule, are songs of night rather than pursuit.

He protects the muse, for at any moment she might reveal the secret that he needs. As a poet he realizes the importance of continuity, of evolving. The craft & passion are his. The art is still to come. That's the final mask, the persona, his face requires.

"At the moment the kids favor the English sound and the folk-rock songs of Bob Dylan, who will probably earn a million dollars over the next eighteen months."

> *Newsweek*: Oct 11/1965

---

[23] "When not in New York City or California, Bob Dylan lives in his manager's mansion in Woodstock. New York. 'I'm writing now for the people who share my feelings.' says Bob. 'The point is not understanding what I write but feeling it. I never wanted to write topical songs, the real me is in my albums *Bringing It All Back Home* and *Highway 61 Revisited*. I wrote topical songs because it was my big chance. In the Village there was a little publication called Broadside and with a topical song you could get in there. I wasn't getting far with the things I was doing, songs like I'm writing now, but Broadside gave me a start.'" (*Hit Parader*: May, 1966).

Part 6 / THE RITES

The choice is three-fold:
       to observe,
       to judge,
       to create,
— but each step leads into the next until you stop stepping & start dancing, chasing your tail around & around until, perhaps, you spiral into eternity.

. . . .

—Oh it doesn't matter what you wear
Just as long as you are there.
So come on every guy, grab a girl.
There'll be dancing in the street.

They're dancing in the street.
This is an invitation.
Across the nation,
A chance for folks to meet.
There'll be laughin', singin' and music swingin'
Dancing in the street.
. . .
Let's form a big boss line.
Yeah, that's fine.
We're dancing in the street.
There's nothing else to do.
Me and you,
We're dancing in the street.
              Dancing In The Street / Sung by Martha & the Vandellas

FIELD TRIP
A ROLLING STONES CONCERT
AT CIVIC AUDITORIUM: MAY 14th 1965

3	F	2
Sec.	Row	Seat

M A I N   F L O O R

The 4 of us (Tina & I, the Hawleys[24]) take a Yellow Cab, Guy's cab, & we're all in good spirits.

None of us have ever been to a rock & roll concert.

Guy's driving the cab calmly but he's a terror when he's off duty & driving his MG (Golden Gate Park, Lew Welch, 2:30 in the morning. Juiced. Zooming, cornering, skid & screech, rubber stink smoke. Many moons ago.)

We all joke. Bob & Tina pun.

Riding up & down the Jones Street hill until we come to a long stop at California Street.

—Look at all the traffic.

—Yeah. I'll bet everyone's going to the Stone's Concert.

—Nah, says Guy

—They're all going to the Smothers' Brothers Concert at Masonic Auditorium.

—Smothers' Brothers?

—A comedy act. Local boys. They're big here.

—I thought everybody was going to the Rolling Stones Concert,

—Not a chance, says Guy to reassure us.

—We'll probably be the only ones there.

—We'll probably be the oldest ones there.

(A flash vision of a teenage Armageddon blinks on in my skull: armed hordes of leather jacket thugs with bicycle chains, zip guns, switch blade knives clicking in & out on the off-beat.)

—What if we're late?

—They always start late.

I am hoping the concert will reveal the passion of mob religion. My muse must be served says the head's captain. A Nathanael West mob-rape. When a fan is converted, what happens? To whom can he testify? I see the arc of union still divided by an infinite fathom as God's huge paw reaches down to touch Adam's big mitt in the Michelangelo sky on the Sistine Chapel.

---

[24] Purveyors of Oyez press. Publishers of several Meltzer titles, including (almost) *Rock Tao* in 1965. [Ed. Note]

(We left our baby-sitter with a pile of *Rave* magazines — an English rock & roll periodical glutted with information & full-page color photos of the Beatles, Herman & the Hermits, P. J. Proby, Manfred Mann, The Rolling Stones: lead article in one issue WE FIND THE GIRLS WHO WILL MARRY THEM / Could YOU marry a Stone? — & we also left her an assortment of the American magazines, all of this as compensation because she is very sad to hear we were going to the Rolling Stones Concert. — if I would've known, she said, — I would have gone too. I'm crazy about the Stones.)

I tell the Hawleys about who makes Brian Jones' guitar, its model-name & who Mick Jagger's steady girl is & what Bill Wyman's daughter is named etc. because I have been reading up on the group as part of my research for this book.

•

Our seats are 6th row center. Bob figured, as I had, that we'd have to get as close as possible in order to see everything.

As we enter the lobby, a young man in a purple Beatle wig is pacing back & forth holding up a placard: I CHALLENGE CHARLIE WATTS TO A DRUM BATTLE.

(I assume he's the young drummer I'd read about earlier this week in the Chronicle. Out of work, he set up his drums on Market Street in front of Woolworth's & began pounding away — a placard next to him announced that his talents were for hire. His girlfriend was with him & told the reporter that it was hard for him to find work because he was extremely shy but, she added, he was a very talented drummer & would fit well with a rock & roll group. She explained that wearing a purple Beatle wig gave him the confidence he needed to present himself to the public.)

We enter the auditorium. It looks like a basketball court changed for the night into a concert hall. The white circles & numbers on the hardwood floor take on mystic significance as if they were parts of a ceremonial magic ritual.

Pre-teen & teenage girls abound. Like strange birds, they strut & pop thru the audience, talking nervously to friends, laughing, not listening, looking towards the empty stage & the side-doors, stage-left, where the performers will enter from.

The girls are returned to an elemental environment. Like neophyte priestesses, like temple-whores, they are radiant & radiate their highest expectations. Proud & most vulnerable to the adult eye, the girls are dressed in their best clothing — clothes integral with the ceremony: Mod-style dresses, high-waisted; bright shifts; schoolboy tweeds with shirt & tie; white lace stockings; pointy-toed Mod shoes; some wear caps like old-time newsboys wore; others have their hair teased into a pile upon their head with a long braid hanging from it; others have straight long hair, as long as a fairytale princess; others have short straight hair with bangs. Whatever they wear they have given great care to. Proper raiment for this significant event.

In all their temporary & fixed shapes, the girls move about, or sit nervously in their seats, or, in groups, try to steal empty front-row seats. Tall & skinny girls with stork-like grace; short, fat girls whose body profiles are like koalas; girls with timeless faces made more lovely by the adult aware of time: their soft skin, the golden down upon their cheeks;

& girls of classic plainness, with cheap plastic cameras around their necks, act as faithful shadows & sheepdogs to more glamorous friends; — all the girls carry themselves with a proprietary dignity fully aware that this sacred event is, above all, theirs.

The sound of the crowd is a surf-like murmur. More people enter the hall, take their seats. A boy & his date sit in their expensive 2nd row seat. ROLLING STONES FOREVER is sewn into the back of his fatigue jacket.

A trio of girls ejected from hi-jacked front-row seats by an usher, pass by their seats in the back; one of the girls says: It's always the undeserving people who get the best seats.

Each to his own costume of self-creation: apprentice beatnik (Dharma Bum) in funky army surplus jacket, worn-out Levis, sandals, a Greco-Roman hairdo, a wispy blond sailor's hornpipe beard;

the surfer boys (Noble Surfer) with dyed-blond hair hanging over their sun-browned face looking like Carl Sandburg;

the budding square with traditional crewcut, short-sleeved shirt, wristwatch;

the Beatle boys with Beatle haircuts in tight Beatle pants & Beatle-style collarless sport-coats wearing Beatle boots;

the young responsibles wearing badges & buttons to signify their particular responsibility: C.O.R.E., S.N.C.C., S.D.S., "Keep the Beatles alive in '65", the peace-button with its forked sign of salvation,—one boy wears a green button with "Peyote" printed in black upon it;

in leather jackets, suede jackets with fleece lined collars & piling, welder's jackets, ranch-boss range-jackets, lumberman jackets, WW II soldier combat jackets;

& they look around at the others to see what the others are, where they're at by the symbology of clothing;

& I notice scattering of peoples representing the 20-30 year old group & they don't look much different than the kids. They wear similar clothing & hairdos, but they are cooler![26] & sit quietly in their chairs.

At 8:53 the audience starts whistling & clapping & stamping their feet for the concert to begin.

—They're so creepy, a young girl says to a boy who is a schoolmate.

(She is smiling at him, attempting to connive him out of his prized seat, which is in the row before us.)

—Who's creepy? he asks.

—The Rolling Stones. They're so creepy. I saw Brian up close when they got off the plane. Brian's so ugly he's cute, ya' know.

Stage-hands move a group of amplifiers & an electric organ onto the stage. Applause from the audience.

The stage-hands finish their work & leave the stage. Applause from the audience that turns into foot-stomping when nothing more happens on the stage.

At last the stage lights are lit & Tony Bigg, a KYA disc-jockey, saunters onto the boards, chewing gum, to announce the first group of the evening: The Marauders from Fresno who are 5 boys looking no older than 17. They wear short-sleeved, wide blue striped shirts & straw colored Levis. The first chord they hit sends a vibration from stage thru the floor that goes right into my colon.

The Marauders are Beach Boys facsimiles & perform many of the Beach Boys' current hits (*Help Me Rhonda*; *Dance, Dance, Dance*; *Fun, Fun, Fun*; Etc.) The rhythm & lead guitarists use their Fender[25] guitars like phallic emblems, swinging them up, thrusting them around, ramming them towards the audience. Yet because they are so young there is nothing vulgar about their pretense.

When they are through, the stage lights are dimmed & the stagehands come out to remove the Marauder's equipment & to bring out the next group's gear.

Tony Bigg announces the next group as Gary Wagner & The Nightbeats[26] — of whom we'll be hearing a lot of in the future, says Tony (chewing gum) because their first single has just been issued.

Gary Wagner is a very pale, lean young man in a soft black leather suit & a chartreuse shirt. His hair is very long & straight becoming nervously curly as it reaches its end. He plays guitar. His group, The Nightbeats, consist of a drummer elevated on top of a raised platform above the group & an electric-bass player. Both men look like 1930 prototypes for the Bowery Boys. The electric bassist looks like a husky Huntz Hall

Gary Wagner & The Nightbeats start the set singing their newly released single.

Gary switches to the electric organ to sing his next number. But the organ doesn't work. A technical disorder. There are illimitable possibilities Gary's loan face lightens as he stands before the malfunctioning organ. Then he turns his back to us to dig about in the instrument's innards, frantically attempting to locate the flaw.

Gary goes back to the organ's keyboard & plays a chord. No sound. His pale face colors slightly & his eyes look out at the audience as if perhaps to see that they are not really before him, watching his prolonged agony. This moment is a dream-fragment. He stands there, staring out.

A member of another group gets on stage & fiddles around with some tubes in the organ's amplifier which seems to correct the problem. Gary plays a chord & the chord is

---

[25] The Fender Co. produces the most popular solid-body electrical guitar. Its peg-head resembles, the head of a penis. Many musicians play the guitar at hip level thus heightening the sexual allusion.

[26] Manuscript galleys list this band as "Gary Wagner & The"; while there appears to be no known record of a band by this name, Gary Wagner of Stockton, CA did form the band Gary Wagner & The Nightbeats [Ed. Note]

heard loudly. The audience applauds. Gary Wagner & The Nightbeats sing their second song.

Their third number features The Nightbeat's drummer who looks like a diminutive Caryl Chessman. The electric-bass player switches to guitar & starts hacking out chords in a way that immediately indicts him as a novice. The drummer begins to sing his specialty-song, *Hot Buttered Buns*, but the long-nozzled mike on his platform distorts his voice & makes it sound as if he were singing in another room thru a torn loudspeaker. Bravely, in his big-chance trance, he keeps singing with great relish about going to his girl's house because he can smell . . .

he pauses, keeps drumming & mugging, & then with a homely leer (this number must've knocked 'em out at school or in the cellblock) he flatly & loudly sings — *Hot Buttered . . . BUNS—ss—ss!* shaking his head, his tongue waggling out of his open mouth, rolling his eyes, bashing at the cymbals.

But the sound is terrible & Gary speaks into his own mike imploring the engineer for some help while the bass-player who switched to guitar continues mutilating chords.

They try again. The guitar playing is worse. The sound is worse. Gary's pallor becomes a raging flush. You can see the machinery of his humiliation at work. He begins to hate the Civic Auditorium & the audience before him as much as he hates himself for being so directly implicated in this ruin.

He grits his teeth & turns his back to us, slamming the organ top with a rigid open hand. The guitarist is locked in his chords & keeps at it & the drummer keeps at it & Gary turns again to the audience with his pale face, beads of cold sweat above his upper lip & around his forehead.

The third time for *Hot Buttered Buns* works. But good sound makes the drummer sound worse & he's too frustrated to be enthusiastic about the song & so it is an anti-climax—especially since it's their last number.

•

The groups get better. Amplifiers, drums & electric organs brought onto the stage, used, carried off, replaced, like a movie sequence to denote change of time: the calendar pages turning, turning.

The groups are better but they begin to sound alike, their excellence is derivative. They imitate to the last note the current hit records & it gets dull.

•

After 10:00 & the audience is getting noisier.

We've seen The Notables; The Mojo Men; a group announced as last seen on *Hollywood-a-Go-Go*, a TV show, (a guitar player stayed out-of-tune throughout the entire set), the Vejtables whose English accents matched the English sound they've mastered & whose drummer was a girl with bangs to her eyebrows & red velvet ribbon around her head —

(at one point, a group of people in the balcony began swaying & clapping & some of

140

them danced in the aisles, but security — guards stopped it quickly).

Paul Revere & The Raiders came charging out dressed in Washington's Army costumes, wearing tri-cornered hats. At one staged moment, Paul Revere's guitar player & saxophone player engaged in symbolic coitus: the phallic Fender gear head rhythmically thrust into the round bell of the saxophone — another well-choreographed occasion had guitarist & saxophonist dancing atop two of the large Vox Super Beatle amplifiers — another crowd-pleaser was when the guitarist played his guitar behind his back — the organ player demonstrated the correct way to play electric organ with elbows, knuckles, fists, knees & finally to use your chin vigorously so that your long hair has a chance to fluff up & down like a parachute; — when Paul Revere & The Raiders were finished, Paul Revere threw a handful of miniature tri-cornered hats into the audience.

•

Now the sound of the audience is the sound of anticipation; a sound of suspense, of a collective throat-clearing; a growling of earth on its axis; of telephone wires & electric lines in damp nights on empty streets: a crackling noise; people are constantly moving around, leaving their seats, taking pictures, the girls keep trying to get at the door next to the stage where the performers enter to the stage.

•

My wife Tina comes back from the ladies room & reports that there are 15 to 20 young girls in it, primping before the mirrors, waiting for the Rolling Stones to go on. Divine hand-maidens elect themselves.

•

The Byrds are the last group before the Rolling Stones. The audience cheers them loudly. Their 1st hit record, *Mr. Tambourine Man* written by Bob Dylan, is on the Top 10 on local record sales charts. Several young girls rush to the stage but are stopped by the special ushers.

The lead-singer, Jim McGuinn, stands at the far end of stage-right. He wears Ben Franklin square-rimmed shades & sings as if his jaw were wired together — his mouth constantly distorted as he pushes & squeezes the words out. They're dressed in anti-uniform uniforms: the tambourine player, Gene Clark, wears Levis, a Levi jacket & resembles Jean-Louis Barrault; David Crosby, rhythm guitar, wears a striped long-sleeved T-shirt, leather vest, tight pants; the drummer looks like the Dutch boy off the Dutch Boy Paint can — his long blonde hair is cut in a hip Buster Brown do.

Much of their excellence is lost in the noise of the audience — girls run down the aisles, flash bulbs; — extra ushers constantly clearing the aisles of the back-seat crowd who, en bloc, move down the aisles to camp on the floors, blocking vision, & people in their seats telling them to sit down, clear the aisle! & girls excitedly talking about the performance going on until they are laughing & squealing & being loudly quieted by members of the audience around them.

The Byrds sing on a stage that is now cluttered with agents, photographers, stage-hands, ushers, security guards — photographers like commandos scuttle around the stage aiming telephoto lenses — girls with transistor radios; girls with transistor tape-recorders giving up their plans to document the concert; the crowd is no longer interested in anything but the main-event.

•

"Big Daddy" Tom Donahue, a portly, bearded disc-jockey, steps onto the stage & announces in a rich, solemn voice that if the audience does not quiet down & clear the aisles, the Rolling Stones will not appear. He reminds us of a black day in Washington when the Rolling Stones were forced to leave the stage after one song because the audience was so unruly. (The audience moans & begins quieting down.) It doesn't make any difference, he explains, whether or not they perform, they'll still get paid.

"Big Daddy" asks the security guards & policemen to come forward to guard the stage. I turn around to look at the 6 security guards & 1 policeman who stand at the back of the auditorium, at ease, & unmoving. "Big Daddy" asks them again to please come up front. Finally they come & some of them get upon the stage, while the others stand before it. They are augmented by group of special ushers. The security guards all look to be in their mid-50s & one of them looks like it might be his last night on the force before retiring tomorrow on his pension. With this show of force, "Big Daddy" brings on the Rolling Stones. The shock of their physical presence silences the audience for a half-second before they give out with a dome-exploding yell.

Before they start their 1st song, the aisles are filled with the girls, ecstatic, flashing their cameras, straining to be seen, waving, weeping & screaming.

"Big Daddy" gets back on the stage & screams into the mike to warn the mob to clear the aisles & no more disturbances or the show will be over. The girls return to their chairs, herded by the ushers.

The Rolling Stones begin.

—*Time is on my side (yes it is)*
  Time is on my side (yes it is)

The lead-singer is Mick Jagger who plays no instrument. His hair is long, his lips are full (—He looks like a frog! a girl squeals) & he moves with a full-awareness of his male function. He is seducing his audience, moving his body, swaying, hip-thrusting, finger snapping.

—*You searchin' for a good time,*
  But you just wait and see,
  You'll came running back.
  (I won't have to worry no more.)

More personnel clutter the stage. The audience is getting louder, gathering its courage, summoning up the Alamo defense spirit; — girls begin edging back down the aisles in packs as guards, ushers & policemen spread out to form a barrier to the stage.

—*Go ahead and have a good time,*
  Ah, baby, do everything your heart desires.
  Remember. I'll always be around.

They come like guerillas, like archers scaling castle walls, rushing down aisles until the aisles are a solid mass of people; charging girls screaming their delight, laughing, crying, talking to the Cosmos, pinching each other, repeating a ritual word over & over & over

—Mick Mick Mick Mick Mick

his voice is no longer heard. It is the sound of the crowd. Just the guitars & drums can be heard accompanying the audience. (& it no longer is important, the girls know the words to all the songs)
  Brian Jones, a fragile-looking youth, has long blonde hair to his shoulders & plays rhythm guitar

—Brian Brian Brian Brian Brian

his blue eyes rest in puffy eye pouches — he looks as if he has just arisen from a deep sleep.

—Oh he's so beautiful so beautiful Oh look at him!

he smiles lovingly & remotely at the Medusa mob before him & flicks the tip of his tongue between his lips which causes a head-cleaving Shriek.

—I love you Charlie I LOVE YOU I LOVE YOU oh Charlie Charlie Charlie

They are beginning to assault the stage & are being pushed back by the officers & ushers

—Oh Keith Keith smile smile here I am

one usher starts clapping his hands in time with the music and gets some of the audience to clap with him, to divert their frenzy;

a pretty girl through a miracle of devotion & God-arranged gravity gets on the stage & throws herself at Bill Wyman, the electric bass-player who chews gum while he plays. The weeping, adoring girl is peeled off of Wyman who, through it all, looks straight ahead, keeps playing & doesn't miss a chew;

a blonde girl in her Mod-style dress (— was she one of the girls in the ladies room priming for this moment, this sacrifice?) breaks thru the barrier & onto the stage to claw into Mick Jagger like a hawk to a rabbit — & he keeps singing as she is yanked away by the old security guard whose age-freckled hand she bites &, while being dragged off-stage, she loses one of her shoes. The old guard returns to his post licking his bitten hand.

We stand on the seats of our chairs in order to see the stage because the whole audience is standing, or they are in the aisles. Looking down at the audience is quite a sensation:

—faces absorbed in intense anguish of not being able to reach their gods; black streaks of eyeliner in the salty wash; a girl behind us has been screaming since the Stones came on —earlier I told her to scream softer which she did for a few seconds but then went back to her red-alert holler — I watch the audience from my chair & it is like being in an airplane flying above a dense pack of clouds.

Keith Richard, lead guitar player, ducks a heavy object thrown at him from a fan but keeps playing.

The Rolling Stones, unafraid, continue singing & playing.

Another blonde girl broad-jumps onto the stage &, yelling triumphantly, grabs ahold of the drummer, Charlie Watts. It takes two guards to haul her off stage, so violent is her response to her rude removal from sacred ground.

Standing on my chair, the mob packed together, celebrating, worshipping, their yelling roaring screaming wailing returns me to a sense of the god-realm: I see them turned into centaurs & flies, goats & griffins, larks & leopards, peacocks & phoenix, snails & scorpions, woodpeckers & unicorns — (which makes me remember a morning in Big Sur when it was early & I walked to a brook to cool my feet & to splash my face so I could wash off the sleep in its skin & upon ferns were groups of muddy-colored triangles which I didn't understand nor recognize (because I live in cities) & I shook a fern branch & stood back: a small group of Monarch butterflies spread their orange, black-bordered wings & took flight up into the clear blue sky — their wings like stained-glass windows the sun shines thru)

By a surprise of misdirection, the Rolling Stones vanish from the stage immediately following their song. Those girls closest to the exit/entrance door are so stunned at the speed of escape that they cannot move until it is too late. The doors clank shut & are barred from within. The rest of the audience is unsure as to whether it is over or not.

It is.

The people start leaving, — girls climb on stage to scavenge sacred relics: a cigarette butt smoked by a Rolling Stone or a button torn off of Mick's jacket — some evidence, some memento.

We pass three teen-age girls seated together in an empty row of seats. They are embracing each other, weeping uncontrollably. Sobbing like 3 widows at a wake, their sorrow is so large, their loss so great, all they can do is hold to each other & let it come forth. One of them looks up, her eyes red-rimmed, to see me watching her cry & I turn away, sorry to have intruded upon her grief of gods who die as quickly as they are born. The concert is over.

ADDENDUMS

[*David included several addendums with the 1965 Rock Tao galleys; however, some are extraneous to the main text. Yet these two discographical checklists and single bibliographical list are of particular interest as they amply demonstrate David's omnivorous nature. Many of us who knew him felt as if he already had read and listened to just about everything ever written or recorded relative to any given subject, but he was ever eager to hear and talk about it all some more. He was always learning. Obviously, as David notes, these lists are not "definitive" (even less so after so many years) but for "the divine scholar-fanatic" they lay out a clear course for further development.*]

ADDENDUM 1

DISCOGRAPHICAL CHECKLIST #1

Nota: This list is a personal selection of long-playing record albums that are, in most cases, still available. It does not attempt to be definitive. That is the work of the divine scholar-fanatic who, I am sure, is readying himself for the task.

Animals, The. THE ANIMALS..MGM 4264
——. ON TOUR...MGM 4281
Baker, LaVern. LA VERN...ATLANTIC 8002
——. BLUES & BALLADS...ATLANTIC 8030
Beach Boys, The. SURFIN' U.S.A...................................CAPITOL T-1890
——. LITTLE DEUCE COUPE..CAPITOL T-1998
——. ALL SUMMER LONG...CAPITOL T-2110
——. TODAY! ....CAPITOL T-2269
——. SUMMER DAYS ....CAPITOL T-235
Beatles, The. INTRODUCING THE BEATLES..................VEEJAY 1092
——. MEET THE BEATLES...CAPITOL T-2047
——. THE BEATLES' SECOND ALBUM ....CAPITOL T-2080
——. SOMETHING NEW ....CAPITOL T-2108
——. A HARD DAY'S NIGHT.......................................UA 3366
——. BEATLES '65...CAPITOL T-2228
——. BEATLES VI..CAPITOL T-2358
——. EARLY BEATLES...CAPITOL T-2309
——. HELP!...CAPITOL MAS-2386
——. RUBBER SOUL...CAPITOL T-242
Berry, Chuck. AFTER SCHOOL...................................CHESS 1426
——. ONE DOZEN BERRYS..CHESS 1432
——. ON STAGE..CHESS 1480

——. CHUCK BERRY'S GREATEST HITS..................…........CHESS 1485

——. ST. LOUIS TO LIVERPOOL............................CHESS 1488

——. CHUCK BERRY IN LONDON..........................CHESS 1495

Big Bopper. CHANTILLY LACE.......................MERCURY 20402

Brown, James. THE AMAZING JAMES BROWN..............KING 743

——. PRISONER OF LOVE.......................................KING 851

——. PURE DYNAMITE!.............................:...............:..KING 883

——. GRITS & SOUL ....SMASH 27057

Bostic, Earl. THE BEST OF BOSTIC..............................KING 500

——. LET'S DANCE WITH BOSTIC ....KING 529

Bradshaw, Tiny. THE GREAT COMPOSER.....................KING 635

Byrds, The. MR. TAMBOURINE MAN …..............COLUMBIA CL 2372

Chad & Jeremy. BEFORE & AFTER.......................COLUMBIA CL 237

Charles, Ray. ROCK & ROLL.......................................ATLANTIC 8002

——. IN PERSON ....ATLANTIC 8039

——. GENIUS SINGS THE BLUES.............................ATLANTIC 8052

——. THE GENIUS OF RAY CHARLES..:...................... ATLANTIC 1312

——. LIVE CONCERT...ABC 500

Checker, Chubby. TWIST!.................................PARKWAY P-7001

Clark V, The Dave. COAST TO COAST …..................EPIC LN-24128

Clark, Petula. DOWNTOWN...................................…WARNER 1590

——. I KNOW A PLACE ....WARNER 1598

Clovers, The. THE CLOVERS.................................ATLANTIC 8009

Cooke, Sam. THE BEST OF SAM COOKE: VOL. I.…........RCA LPM-262

——. THE BEST OF SAM COOKE: VOL. II.......................RCA LPM-3373

Dick & Dee Dee. THOU SHALT NOT STEAL...............……WARNER 1586

Diddley, Bo. BO DIDDLEY.....................................….......CHECKER 1431

——. GO, GO, BO DIDDLEY ....CHECKER 1436

——. BO DIDDLEY IS A LOVER.......................…....(Lack of Information)

——. BO DIDDLEY'S A TWISTER ....CHECKER 2962

——. HAVE GUITAR, WILL TRAVEL.....................……......CHECKER 2674

——. BO DIDDLEY'S A GUNSLINGER..............…....…..(Lack of Information)

——. BEACH PARTY ....:.........................CHECKER 2988

——. 16 ALL-TIME HITS ....CHECKER 2989

——. HEY, GOOD LOOKIN' ....CHECKER 2992

——. TWO GREAT GUITARS (W/ CHUCK BERRY)…......CHECKER 2991

Domino, Fats. 12,000,000 RECORDS ....IMPERIAL 9061

——. ROCK & ROLLIN' (A 2 record set) ....IMPERIAL 9004, 9007

Drifters, The. ROCKIN' & DRIFTIN'..................................ATLANTIC 8022

——. OUR BIGGEST HITS……........................…............ATLANTIC 8093

Dylan, Bob. BOB DYLAN ....COLUMBIA CL-1779

——. THE FREEWHEELIN' BOB DYLAN ....COLUMBIA CL-1986
——. TIMES THEY ARE A CHANGIN' ....COLUMBIA CL-2105
——. ANOTHER SIDE OF BOB DYLAN ....COLUMBIA CL-2193
——. BRINGING IT ALL BACK HOME...................COLUMBIA CL-2528
——. HIGHWAY 61 REVISITED ....COLUMBIA CL-2389
Everly Brothers, The. THE EVERLY BROTHERS.....CADENCE CLP-3003
——. SONGS OUR DADDY TAUGHT US.................CADENCE CLP-3016
——. A DATE WITH THE EVERLY BROTHERS...   ....WARNER 1395
——. TOP VOCAL DUET..WARNER 1418
——. GREAT COUNTRY HITS..WARNER 1513
——. ROCK 'N' SOUL ....WARNER 1578
——. GONE, GONE, GONE.................................. ......WARNER 1585
Fontana, Wayne & the Mindbenders. GAME OF LOVE... FONTANA 27542
Four Seasons, The. RAG DOLL ....PHILLIPS 200146
——. THE 4 SEASONS TO ENTERTAIN YOU...........PHILLIPS 200164
Freddie & the Dreamers. HEY!...MERCURY 21017
——. DO THE "FREDDIE"...MERCURY 21026
Freed, Alan. ROCK AROUND THE CLOCK....................CORAL 57213
Gore, Lesley. BOYS!!...MERCURY 20901
——. GIRL TALK...MERCURY 20943
——. LESLEY GORE'S GOLDEN HITS........…….....MERCURY 21024
Haley, Bill & the Comets. ROCK AROUND THE CLOCK....DECCA 8225
——. ROCK & ROLL STAGE SHOW.……............….........DECCA 8345
——. ROCKIN' THE JOINT...DECCA 8775
Herman's Hermits. HERMAN'S HERMITS.................….........MGM 4285
    HERMAN'S HERMITS ON TOUR.............................…...MGM 4295
Holly, Buddy. BUDDY HOLLY.......................................CORAL 57210
——. THE BUDDY HOLLY STORY (A 2 record set).CORAL 57279/57326
——. BUDDY HOLLY WITH THE CRICKETS.............…...CORAL 57405
Hollyridge Strings, The. THE BEATLES SONG BOOK ....CAPITOL T-2116
——. THE BEATLES SONG BOOK: VOL. II ....CAPITOL T-2202
——. HIT SONGS OF ELVIS PRESLEY............................CAPITOL T-2221
Hooker, John Lee. SINGS THE BLUES....................CROWN CLP 5232
——. FOLK BLUES ....CROWN CLP 5295
——. THE BIG SOUL OF JOHN LEE HOOKER..................VEEJAY 1058
Hopkins, Lightnin'. SINGS THE BLUES........................CROWN CLP 5224
——. LIGHTNIN' SAM HOPKINS ....ARHOOLIE F-1011
——. EARLY RECORDINGS...........................ARHOOLIE R-2007
Howlin' Wolf. SINGS THE BLUES.......................CROWN CLP 5240
——. MOANIN' IN THE MOONLIGHT.........................CHESS 1434
——. HOWLIN' WOLF ....CHESS 1469

Impressions, The. PEOPLE GET READY............................ABC 505
——. GREATEST HITS...ABC 515
Isley Brothers, The. SHOUT!..RCA LPM-2156
——. TWIST & SHOUT...…...WAND 653
——. TWISTING & SHOUTING ....UA 3313
Jan & Dean. THE GOLDEN HITS OF..................................LIBERTY 3248
——. LITTLE OLD LADY FROM PASADENA.............LIBERTY 1377
King, B. B. LIVE AT THE REGAL.....................................…..ABC 509
Kinks, The. KINKS-SIZE.......................................REPRISE 6158
Lee, Brenda. BRENDA LEE...…...DECCA 4039
Lewis, Gary & The Playboys. GARY LEWIS..................LIBERTY 3408
Lewis, Jerry Lee. THE JERRY LEE LEWIS SHOW.....…....SMASH 27056
——. RETURN OF ROCK...SMASH 27063
Little Anthony & the Imperials. LITTLE ANTHONY.................DCP 3801
——. GOIN' OUT OF MY HEAD..…..DCP 3808
Little Richard. HERE'S LITTLE RICHARD.................SPECIALTY 2100
——. LITTLE RICHARD ....SPECIALTY 2103
——. LITTLE RICHARD IS BACK.............................…....VEEJAY 1107
Little Walter. THE BEST OF LITTLE WALTER.................CHESS 1428
Lopez, Trini. TRINI LOPEZ AT P.J.'S...........................…...REPRISE 6093
Mann, Manfred. MANFRED MANN.............................…...ASCOT 13015
——. THE 5 FACES OF MANFRED MANN......................ASCOT 13018
Martha & The Vandellas. MEMORIES............................GORDY 228
——. HEATWAVE...…...GORDY 907
Marvelelles. LIVE ON STAGE.....................................…......TAMLA 241
McPhattcr, Clyde & the Drifters. LIVE AT THE APOLLO..MERCURY 20915
  ——. ROCK & ROLL...…..ATLANTIC 8003
Miracles, The. HI..…..TAMLA 220
——. DOIN' MICKEY'S MONKEY...............................…..TAMLA 245
Nashville Teens, The. THE NASHVILLE TEENS....….........LONDON 3407
Nelson, Ricky. MILLION SELLERS............................…IMPERIAL 9232
Orbison, Roy. GREATEST HITS............................…......MONUMENT 8000
——. IN DREAMS..…...MONUMENT 8003
——. EARLY ROY ORBISON............................…........MONUMENT 8293
——. MORE GREATEST HITS OF ROY ORBISON......MONUMENT 8024
Orlons, The. ALL THE ORLONS' HITS............................…...CAMEO l033
Peter & Gordon. A WORLD WITHOUT LOVE................CAPITOL T-2115
Phillips, Esther. ROCK & ROLL....................................ATLANTIC 8102
——. SINGS COUNTRY & WESTERN HITS...........…...(Lack of Information)
——, REFLECTIONS OF COUNTRY WESTERN GREATS...(multiple issues)
Pickett, Wilson. TOO LATE..…..DOUBLE L-2300

Pitney, Gene. THE MANY SIDES OF GENE PITNEY..........MUSICOR 2001

——. GEORGE JONES & GENE PITNEY……...…….……MUSICOR 2044

Platters, The. 10th ANNIVERSARY ALBUM.................MERCURY 20933

Presley, Elvis. BLUE SUEDE SHOES……………...............RCA LPM 1254

——. ELVIS ……………………………………………………RCA LPM 1382

——. ELVIS PRESLEY'S GOLDEN RECORDS: VOL. 1……...RCA LPM 1707

——. FOR LP FANS ONLY…………………………………..RCA LPM 2011

——. A DATE WITH ELVIS……………...……………….…..RCA LPM 2011

Proby, P. J. SOMEWHERE ....LIBERTY 3406

Ray, Johnnie. JOHNNIE RAY'S BIGGEST HITS……….COLUMBIA CL 1227

Redding, Otis. OTIS REDDING……………………………….ATCO 33-161

——. SOUTH BALLADS……………………………………...VOLT 411

Reed, Jimmy. I'M JIMMY REED……………………………VEEJAY 1004

——. ROCKIN' WITH REED…………………………………...VEEAY 1008

——. FOUND LOVE…………………………………………VEEJAY 1022

——. NOW APPEARING …………………………………….VEEJAY 1025

——. JIMMY REED AT CARNEGIE HALL (A 2 record set)…...VEEJAY 1035

——. THE BEST OF JIMMY REED……………………………..VEEJAY 1039

——. JUST JIMMY REED………………………………….VEEJAY 1050

Righteous Brothers, The. THE RIGHTEOUS BROTHERS..MOONGLOW 1001

——. YOU'VE LOST THAT LOVING FEELING………....MOONGLOW 5266

Revere, Paul & the Raiders. HERE THEY COME!.............COLUMBIA CL-2307

Rolling Stones, The. THE ROLLING STONES…………........…..LONDON 3375

——. 12 x 5 …………………………………………….LONDON 3402

——. NOW…..LONDON 3420

——. OUT OF OUR HEADS …………….................,…, …….LONDON 3429

Sam the Sham & the Pharaohs. WOOLY BULLY.......................MGM 4297

Searchers, The. MEET THE SEARCHERS……………………….KAPP 1363

——. THIS IS US...KAPP 1409

Shangri-Las, The. LEADER OF THE PACK…………….REDBIRD RB 20—1011

Shirelles, The. GOLDEN OLDIES……………………………….SCEPTER 516

SING & PLAY ALONG BEATLE KIT…………………...…….LONDON 3403

Sonny & Cher. LOOK AT US……………………………….ATCO 33-177

Springfield, Dusty. OOOOOWEEEE!!!...............................PHILLIPS 200 I 74

Staple Singers. UNCLOUDY DAY………………………….VEEJAY 5000

——. WILL THIS CIRCLE BE UNBROKEN?…………………VEEJAY 5008

——. SWING LOW……………………………………..VEEJAY 5014

——. THE BEST OF THE STAPLE SINGERS………………...VEEJAY 5019

——. HAMMER & NAILS …………………………………RIVERSIDE 1501

——. AMEN!... EPIC LN-24132

Supremes, The. MEET THE SUPREMES……………………MOTOWN 606

——. A BIT OF LIVERPOOL…………………………………MOTOWN 623

Tex, Joe. HOLD WHAT YOU'VE GOT………..…………..ATLANTIC 8106

——. HOLD ON……………………………………………CHECKER 2993

Them. HERE COMES THE NIGHT ……………………....PARROT 61005

Treniers, The. SOUVENIR ALBUM…………………..……...DOT 3257

Twitty, Conway. CONWAY TWITTY……………………....METRO 512

Unit 4+2. NUMBER 1………………………………...……LONDON 3247

Ventures. THE FABULOUS VENTURES…………………....DOLTON 2029

Vinton, Bobby. MR. LONELY……………………………EPIC LN-24136

Walker, T-Bone. T-BONE WALKER………………………CAPITOL T-1958

——. SINGS THE BLUES…………………………………IMPERIAL 9098

——. I GET SO WEARY…………………………………IMPERIAL 9146

Warwick, Dionne. PRESENTING DIONNE WARWICK………SCEPTER 508

——. ANYONE WHO HAD A HEART…………………………SCEPTER 517

——. MAKE WAY FOR DIONNE WARWICK……………......SCEPTER 523

——. THE SENSITIVE SOUND OF DIONNE WARWICK…...SCEPTER 528

Waters, Muddy, THE BEST OF MUDDY WATERS……………..CHESS 1427

——. AT NEWPORT ....CHESS 1449

——. MUDDY WATERS: FOLKSINGER…………………….CHESS 1483

Watson, Johnny "Guitar". JOHNNY "GUITAR" WATSON. …….CHESS 1490

Yardbirds, The. FOR YOUR LOVE...EPIC LN-24167

Zombies, The. SHE'S NOT THERE………………..PARAMOUNT 61001

ADDENDUM 2

DISCOGRAPHICAL CHECKLIST #2

Nota: This is perhaps a more personalized selection of records: These musicians & musics have affected the musical forms of today in as much as I have been affected by them & can see (hear) their influence in what is currently popular & new.

AMERICAN SKIFFLE BANDS...FOLKWAYS 2610
ANGOLA PRISONERS' BLUES.....................................FOLK-LYRIC 3
ANTHOLOGY OF AMERICAN FOLK MUSIC
     (A 6 record set) ....FOLKWAYS 2951/53
BALLADS & SONGS...OLD TIMEY 102
BLUES IN THE MISSISSIPPI NIGHT.........................UNITED ARTISTS 797
BLUES 'N TROUBLE, Vol. 1 ....ARHOOLIE F-1006
——. Ibid, Vol. 2..ARHOOLIE F-1012
Carter Family, The. THE FAMOUS CARTER FAMILY..........HARMONY 7280
Cotton, Elizabeth. NEGRO FOLG SONGS & TUNES.............FOLKWAYS 3526
THE COUNTRY BLUES, Vol. 1....................................FOLKWAYS RBF 1
——. Ibid, Vol. 2...FOLKWAYS RBF 9
COUNTRY BLUES CLASSICS, Vol. 1...........................BLUES CLASSICS 5
——. Ibid. Vol 2...BLUES CLASSICS 6
Estes, Sleepy John. THE LEGEND OF................................DELMARK 603
——. BROKE & HUNGRY ....DELMARK 608
THE GREAT JUG BANDS ....ORIGIN OJL-4
Guthrie, Woody. BOUND FOR GLORY............................FOLKWAYS 2481
——. DUST BOWL BALLADS...RCA LPV-502
——. LIBRARY OF CONGRESS RECORDINGS (A 3 record set) ELEKTRA 2712
Holiday, Billie. BILLIE HOLIDAY ....MAINSTREAM 56000
——. THE GOLDEN YEARS (A 3 record set)...................COLUMBIA C3L-21
Hurt, Mississippi John. MISSISSIPPI JOHN HURT..................PIEDMONT 13157
——. WORRIED BLUES...PIEDMONT 13161
JAZZ: Vol. 1/THE SOUTH...FOLKWAYS 2801
——. Ibid. Vol. 2/THE BLUES....................................... FOLKWAYS 2802
——. Ibid. Vol. 4/JAZZ SINGERS...................................FOLKWAYS 2804
Johnson, Blind Willie. BLIND WILLIE JOHNSON...............FOLKWAYS 3585
——. 1927-1930 ....FOLKWAYS RBF-10
Johnson, Robert. KING OF THE DELTA SINGERS.......... COLUMBIA CL-1654
JUG, JOOK & WASHBOARD BANDS.........................BLUES CLASSICS 2
Leadbelly. LAST SESSIONS (A 4 record set).....................FOLKWAYS 2941/2

——. LEADBETTER'S BEST ....CAPITOL T-182l

Lewis. Furry. SINGS THE BLUES...................................FOLKWAYS 3825

Louvin Brothers, The. TRAGIC SONGS OF LIFE.......................CAPITOL T-769

Memphis Minnie. MEMPHIS MINNIE.........................BLUES CLASSICS 1

MISSISSIPPI BLUES, THE ....ORIGIN OJL-5

Monk, Thelonious. MONK, Vol. l.................................BLUE NOTE 1510

——. Ibid. Vol. 2.. BLUE NOTE 1511

——. MONK ....PRESTIGE 7159

Monroe, Bill. THE GREAT BILL MONROE ....HARMONY 7290

——. THE MONROE BROTHERS ....CAMDEN 774

——. FATHER OF BLUEGRASS MUSIC............................CAMDEN 719

Parker, Charlie. THE IMMORTAL CHARLIE PARKER.............SAVOY 12001

——. THE GENIUS OF CHARLIE PARKER (2 record set)........SAVOY 12009/14

Pleasure, King. GOLDEN DAYS....................................HI-FI 425

RARE BLUES OF THE 20'S.....................................HISTORICAL ASC-1

REALLY, THE COUNTRY BLUES!....................................ORIGIN OJL-2

Reinhardt, Django. THE BEST OF (2 record set)..............HISTORICAL ASC-1

——. DJANGOLOGY.......................................RCA LPM-2319

——. JAZZ FROM PARIS..VERVE 8015

Rogers, Jimmie. TRAIN WHISTLE BLUES ....RCA LPM-1640

RURAL BLUES, THE (2 record set) ....FOLKWAYS RBF-202

Shankar, Ravi. IN CONCERT......................................WORLD PACIFIC -1421

——. IN LONDON ....WORLD PACIFIC 1430

——. MASTER MUSICIAN ....WORLD PACIFIC 1422

Smith, Bessie. THE BESSIE SMITH STORY
             (4 record set)................COLUMBIA CL-855/8

Watson, Doc. DOC WATSON ....VANGUARD 9152

White, Bukka. BUKKA WHITE..................................TAKOMA 7001

——. SKY SONGS, Vol. 1..ARHOOLIE F-1019

Williams, Hank. HANK WILLIAMS Vol. 1 (3 record set)......................MGM 3-E2

——. Ibid, Vol. 2 (3 record set) ....MGM 3-E4

Williams, Big Joe. BLUES...DELMARK 602

——. TOUGH TIMES...ARHOOLIE F-1002

Williams, Robert Pete. PRISON BLUES.............................FOLK-LYRIC 109

Williamson, Sonny Boy. SONNY BOY WILLIAMSON......BLUES CLASSICS 3

ADDENDUM 3

A Reading List

Anger, Kenneth. HOLLYWOOD BABYLON. Phoenix, 1965
Astrov, Margot, ed. THE WINGED SERPENT, NY, 1946
Bast, William. JAMES DEAN. NY, 1956
Bettelheim, Bruno. SYMBOLIC WOUNDS. NY, 1962, revised ed.
Budge, E. A. Wallis. AMULETS & TALISMANS. NY, 1961
Bunyan, John. THE PILGRIM'S PROGRESS (illus. by William Blake)
Campbell, Joseph. THE HERO WITH 1000 FACES. NY, 1956
——, ed. THE ERANOS YEARBOOKS. NY, 1954-64
Charters, Samuel. THE COUNTRY BLUES. NY, 1959
——. THE POETRY OF THE BLUES. NY, 1963
Cocteau, Jean. THE HAND OF A STRANGER. NY, 1959
Confucius. THE UNWOBBLING PIVOT & THE GREAT DIGEST (trans. Ezra Pound). NY, 1950
——. ANALECTS (trans. Ezra Pound). Washington, nd
DeBlasio, Edward. ALL ABOUT THE BEATLES, NY, 1964
Desmonde, William. MAGIC, MYTH & MONEY. NY, 1962
Eckhart, Meister. WORKS (ed. Pfeiffer). London, 1956
Eliade, Mircea. MYTHS, DREAMS & MYSTERIES. NY, 1960
——. SHAMANISM: ARCHAIC TECHNIQUES OF ECSTASY. NY, 1964
Epstein, Brian. A CELLARFUL OF NOISE. NY, 1964
Ferguson, George. SIGNS & SYMBOLS IN CHRISTIAN ART. NY, 1961
Goldsmith, E. E. LIFE SYMBOLS AS RELATED TO SEX SYMBOLISM. NY, 1924
Goodman, Pete. OUR OWN STORY BY THE ROLLING STONES. NY, 1964
Graves, Robert. THE GREEK MYTHS. NY, 1957
——. THE WHITE GODDESS. NY, 1948
Harding, Esther. WOMAN'S MYSTERIES. NY, 1911
Harrison, Jane. ANCIENT ART & RITUAL. London, 1913
——. EPILEGOMENA TO THE STUDY OF GREEK RELIGION & THEMIS. NY, 1962
——. MYTHOLOGY. NY, 1963
Hoffman, Dezo. THE BEATLE BOOK. NY, 1964
Jung, C. G. 2 ESSAYS ON ANALYTICAL PSYCHOLOGY. NY, 1953
——. MEMORIES, DREAMS, REFLECTIONS. NY, 1963
——. FLYING SAUCERS. NY, 1959
——. w/ Carl Kerenyi. ESSAYS ON A SCIENCE OF MYTHOLOGY. NY 1949

Kerenyi. Carl. THE RELIGION OF THE GREEKS & ROMANS. NY, 1962

Legman, Gershon. LOVE & DEATH. NY, 1949

——. THE HORN BOOK. NY, 1964

McLuhan, Marshall. UNDERSTANDING MEDIA. NY, 1964

Macchioro, Vittorio. FROM ORPHEUS TO PAUL. NY, 1930

Morin, Edgar. THE STARS. NY, 1960

Neumann, Eric. THE GREAT MOTHER. NY, 2nd ed, 1963

——. THE ORIGINS & HISTORY OF CONSCIOUSNESS. NY, 2nd ed, 1964

Oliver, Paul. BLUES FELL THIS MORNING. NY, 1960

——. CONVERSATIONS WITH THE BLUES. NY, 1966

Paracelsus. SELECTED WRITINGS (ed. Jacobi). NY, 2nd ed, 1958

Plotinus. THE SIX ENNEADS. Chicago, 1952

Radin, Paul. THE TRICKSTER. NY, 1956

——. PRIMITIVE RELIGION. NY, 1957

Scholem, Gershom. MAJOR TRENDS IN JEWISH MYSTICISM. NY, 1961

Shepard, Billy. THZ TRUE STORY OF THE BETTLES. NY, 1964

Sumrall, Lester F. WORSHIPPERS OF THE SILVER SCREEN. Minneapolis, 1930

Seyffert, Oskar. DICTIONARY OF CLASSICAL ANTIQUITIES. NY, 1963

Sinclair, M. & Chang, Lily Pau-Hu, trans. THE POEMS OF TAO CH'IEN. Honolulu, 1953

Underhill, Ruth. SINGING FOR POWER. Berkeley, 1938

Westman, H. THE SPRINGS OF CREATIVITY. NY, 1961

Wilhelm, Richard, trans. THE I CHING. NY, 1952

AFTERWORD

TONAL AURA: DAVID MELTZER AND THE POETICS OF COLLAGE

by Marina Lazzara

History is a creative act of the present.
–Chris Carlsson, Shaping San Francisco[1]

David in my apartment near the plywood desk reciting *When I Was a Poet*[2]. My dog at his feet and the tiny Victorian studio filled like a concert hall. Kids there with ears able to grasp city imagery. The everyday. The adults in the grey area between the lines, in the hallway. He reads from the book but in conversation with us, storytelling. Legacy and laughter.

*

I attend a house reading with David. The host has no real interest in poetry or jazz. He is offering his home to his poet friend. David scans the bookshelf as we enter. As we hang our coats, David finds an endearing way to include the host. At dinner, during a moment of poets chewing, he asks about the man's interest in fishing, which baits he prefers, which hooks. The child of a comedic writer, David hooks a word play or two about a big catch. Tossing back the injured. The poets talk fishing.

*

David was a mirror and a receptor, a reflector and a sponge. He was the ultimate Collagist. One who picks up the pieces, finds gum wrappers and old match books, and glues them together to form a star.

*

In conversation with David, the writer and educator, Christopher Winks, referring to David's editing of the anthologies *Birth*[3], *Death*[4], *Reading Jazz*[5], and *Writing Jazz*[6], describes how "You're making a new work out of all those quotes." David responds, "True. I was inspired by Walter Benjamin's desire to 'write' a book by gathering texts together that told the story he would discover in the collage. He wouldn't have to write anything; instead, he would let fragments cohere into a unified text. *Reading Jazz* used a polyvocal approach in a rigid, polemical way. There was no give or take there, no complexity."[7]

*

I tell David I hate writing prose. It's like pulling a tapeworm from my stomach through my mouth. He says "Everything I write is poetry. There's no difference. If it's all poetry, then let it be. If you hear poetry, then write a poem."

＊

What exhales through the language of David Meltzer's writing, no matter what form it takes, is a collage of perception. A kaleidoscope. Like his dear friend, Wallace Berman's credo: "Art is Love is God". A collage in words itself, whereas collage serves as an analogy, is a reconfiguring of connection, reminiscent of Arthur Rimbaud's "disordering of the senses".

＊

Vision

The heart sees
what the mind sees
what the eyes see

differently [8]

＊

I didn't know David was a musician when I began my studies with him. I didn't know much about him. He seemed like a nerdy scholar with an odd sense of humor and a music buff. A thrifty guy. As a teacher, he never talked about himself, his work. As I got to know him and his life, I discovered the albums *Poet Song* [9] and *Serpent Power* [10]. I began to read the anthologies and the introductions to those books. He was drawing together chopped up pieces of inspiration from his mentors and friends along with his reading and music work; combining all of that with his everyday life as a pedestrian, as a father, as a husband, as a friend, as a teacher, as someone who loves humankind and collects evidence of that love. There was something uniquely inspiring in David's absolute humanism. A poetics.

＊

I work with David on his book *Talking with the Poets* [11]. I record and transcribe the interviews. He calls me several times and leaves the same message until I return his call. "Leave in every *uhm*, every *sigh*, every *like*. Try to capture every mispronounced word. And don't leave out one breath."

＊

In the introduction to *Reading Jazz*, David writes about Charlie Parker:

> Parker's velocity of ideas, references, quotes, rhythmic interplay, suspense, surge, a monologue in dialogic interplay; a person thinking out loud, tapping a huge archive, deeply enmeshed in the language of music, the music of action, action of thought, recall, recombining them in sonic curls and ribbons of music. How easy for me to abstract qualities present in the presence of the player and his music. Each moment heard in memory written. What's left? Something like Walter Benjamin's "aura," a tonal aura substitutes for the music long gone, a ghetto of ghosts made up of words.[12]

*

As a teacher, David's pedagogy was anti-scholarship, where reading and writing is the act of knowledge, not arduous research and bureaucracy. A content treadmill of creation toward a collective history. I am reminded of him as an educator when I read Paulo Freire, the Brazilian educator, author of *Pedagogy of the Oppressed*[13]. Freire believed that through learning knowledge will emerge only through invention and re-invention, through the hopeful inquiry human beings pursue in the world and with each other.

*

David in essay on Paul Celan:

> Who was lost will not be found. They will not speak through children. We dream a reconstructed voice in wire recordings, acetate sandstorm 78s, white discs made in voice-o-gram booths. Lost beyond the voice is the book. The page. The word. *Mi. Mah.* What. Who. Who is lost can not be found. They will not be born. *Aleph bayt kaput.* Files flash-fired into ash. Burnt map of Eden. Missiles of telegram uncoil erupting wild sparking wires. One by one the radios play silence. One by one they go beyond the word.[14]

*

"All myth," David writes in *Rock Tao* "begins as news."

*

David's already in the classroom when the first student arrives. He takes a taxi from the East Bay. Has the same taxi driver every time. He enters and sets up his big bound books that seem heavier than himself, especially in his hobbled existence shortly after hip surgery.

Students assemble. He dissembles the bounded books, pulls out particular pages. They are leaves. They are angels. They are just paper. The students talk that conversation that inevitably gets louder and waves between silence and a sound that becomes murmur, as people make connections or wear off caffeine, fight a bit to be heard over the person behind them.

David looks through his papers patiently, turning, turning over, turning and placing to the left, topping that with another. Slight swaying sounds, slightly winded and soundful pages. He occasionally answers a question or greets someone as people walk to their seats.

He throws torn glossy magazine pages and watches them slide down the table like dinner plates. Automatically, the students pass them down spreading them around the tabletop so they won't cover one another. They are ads for cars, for fashion, ads with high heels and cleavage and lace bras, ads for movies, for insurance, for college degrees, ads for health insurance.

There's a natural lull in conversation as the students help to lay out the pages and then silence. Some breathing. Concentration. David says, "Hello." Then a David giggle which includes a hand to his chin, holding it like the neck of a guitar. "The pages in front of you," there's a bit of a stir in the room. "The pages in front of you are examples of, uhm, poetry. Choose one. Tell me why."

We giggle. Someone says, "You mean anti-poetry." "No," David says. "These advertisements use language and imagery in the same manner as the poet."

David mentions some obvious literary techniques, graphic design, obvious critical thinking analogies. Says, "It can't be dichotomized." One of his catch phrases urging us on to think not only outside the box, but inside the layers of wood that connect the frame, to begin to tear up the pages, to begin to reassemble, kola, collage.

He continues to suggest technique: Rhythm of color. Various seemingly unrelated images brought together designed to influence.

Seduction by visual sound.

[1] http://www.shapings.org/

[2] Meltzer, David. *When I Was A Poet*. Pocket Poets Number 60. (San Francisco: City Lights, 2011)

[3] Meltzer, David, ed. *Birth, an anthology of ancient texts, songs, prayers, and stories.* (San Francisco: North Point Press, 1981).

[4] Meltzer, David, ed. *Death: An Anthology of Ancient Texts, Songs, Prayers and Stories.* (San Francisco: North Point Press, 1984).

[5] Meltzer, David, ed. *Reading Jazz.* (San Francisco: Mercury House, 1993).

[6] Meltzer, David, ed. *Writing Jazz.* (San Francisco: Mercury House, 1993).

[7] Meltzer, David, ed. *San Francisco beat: talking with the poets.* (San Francisco: City Lights Books, 2001): 214-15.

[8] Meltzer, David. *David's Copy: The Selected Poems of David Meltzer.* (New York: Penguin, 2005): 6.

[9] Meltzer, David and Tina. *Poet Song.* Vanguard VSD 6519. 1969.

[10] The Serpent Power. *The Serpent Power.* Vanguard VSD-79252. 1967.

[11] Meltzer, David, ed. *San Francisco beat: talking with the poets.* (San Francisco: City Lights Books, 2001).

[12] *Reading Jazz*, 18.

[13] Freire, Paulo. *Pedagogy of the Oppressed.* Translated by Myra Bergman Ramos. (New York: Bloomsbury Academic, 2012).

[14] authors, various (1983) "Encounters: American Poets on Paul Celan," *Studies in 20th Century Literature*: Vol. 8: 1, Article 8, 26-27.

A LOOK AT DAVID MELTZER

by Julie Rogers

David Meltzer was born in Rochester, New York, in 1937, the oldest and only son of four children, and an older sister from a previous union. From an early age he was raised in Brooklyn by his mother, a former harp prodigy from southern California, and his father, a cellist with the Rochester Philharmonic Orchestra, long employed as a radio comedy writer in New York City who later worked in television out in California. His father's insistence on becoming a "new" Jew, juxtaposed to the religious and cultural influences of his paternal grandparents, seemed to impact David later in life when he took up his intensive study of various religions, with emphasis upon Buddhism, mystical Judaism, and the Kabbalah. He grew up sitting beneath or nearby the grand piano as his mother played, and regularly witnessed live classical music in the front room of their railroad flat in Brooklyn. A realized poet at age 11, David was also a budding musician and said he "endured" his early stage debuts singing and playing guitar for the radio program, *The Horn and Hardart Children's Hour.*

After his parent's marriage ended, as a teen David moved, or "was exiled" as he put it, to the west coast to live with his father in Hollywood. He soon left Fairfax High, worked in a magazine stand on Hollywood Blvd., and became part of Wallace Berman's avant-garde artistic circle. David's own collage art reflects those years, as well as his many friendships within this milieu of southern California artists and writers, and he remained close to George Herms and others from that time until the end of his life. In 1957, David migrated to North Beach in San Francisco, where he began his literary career during the Beat heyday among notable poets and friends such as Allen Ginsberg, Michael McClure, Diane di Prima, Lew Welch, Robert Duncan, and Joanne Kyger. He and SF Poet Laureate Jack Hirschman were close for over sixty years. For a time, he worked at Discovery Bookstore and at the Co-Existence Bagel Shop, and was known to give away free food and sometimes "very discounted books." Alongside Jack Spicer, he also helped run "Blabbermouth Night" at The Place, a renown Beat hang-out in North Beach.

David Meltzer has long been considered a major figure in the San Francisco/Beat Renaissance. He came to prominence as the youngest poet to have work included in Don Allen's famous anthology, *The New American Poetry 1945–1960.* At the age of 20 he recorded *Poet w/Jazz* in Los Angeles, the first of his two CD's. David also became a singer-songwriter, musician (mandolin, banjo, keyboards, and harmonica) and guitarist for several Bay Area bands during the 1960s, along with his first wife, singer Tina Meltzer. He stood in line at the Unemployment Office with Janis Joplin and jammed in North Beach on nights along with David Crosby and other notable 1960s rock figures. His bands included The Snopes, oriented towards bluegrass, and The Serpent Power, his "psychedelic rock" band (who once opened for Jefferson Airplane in San Francisco.) This album is included on *Rolling Stone Magazine's* Top 40 List for 1968. He later recorded additional LPs with Tina, including *Green Morning* and *Poet Song*. They had four children and for a time were residents of the renowned writers and artists haven of Bolinas, California. They later moved to Richmond, California, and after Tina passed, David finally resettled in a small apartment in nearby Oakland, where he lived for the rest of his life.

David Meltzer is the author of many volumes of poetry including *Arrows: Selected Poetry 1957 – 1992, Luna, The Name, Bark: A Polemic, David's Copy: Selected Poems,* and *Beat Thing.* His work is can also be seen in countless literary anthologies. Most recently, the late Les Gottesman's Omerta Publications released three chapbooks: *Stunt Man* in 2013, followed later by *Trading Fours* and *Sharing Breath,* love poems David and I wrote to each other, published posthumously in 2020. He is also known for his fiction, essays, and numerous anthologies and collections of interviews such as *The Secret Garden: An Anthology in the Kabbalah, Reading Jazz, Writing Jazz, Birth, Death,* and three City Lights' titles: *San Francisco Beat: Talking with the Poets, When I Was a Poet,* #60 in City Lights' legendary Pocket Poet Series, and *Two-Way Mirror: A Poetry Notebook,* intended as a textbook for use in schools. His book *No Eyes: Lester Young* (2000), inspired a CD released in 2018 by Italian jazz composer, musician and band leader Emanuele Cisi, titled *No Eyes: Looking at Lester Young.* David was also publisher, editor and an author for Tree Publications, which produced six anthologies of contemporary and celebrated Jewish writings, and more than twenty beautifully designed chapbooks of poetry.

After teaching briefly at San Francisco State University, David taught in the Undergraduate Humanities and Graduate Poetics Programs at the New College of California in San Francisco for thirty years. He also led writing seminars along the west coast and across the country, and was beloved by his students. He taught writing workshops in the California prison system, and had a poetry-oriented radio show on KPFA in the San Francisco Bay Area. He was well known and lauded as an extraordinary performer, and literally could blow anyone off the stage–the mix of his political commentary, profound insight, subliminal philosophy, and matchless comedic charm were unequaled, *and that voice.* For decades he read his work at countless venues in the United States and Europe, but was mostly seen in southern and northern California. In 2008, David received the Foundation for Contemporary Arts Grants to Artists Award. In 2011, he was given the San Francisco Bay Area Guardian's Lifetime Achievement Award, and in 2012 he was nominated for the Northern California Book Award in Poetry. He is featured in several documentary films, including Mary Kerr's epic, *Wild History Groove,* focusing on artists and writers of North Beach in San Francisco. In 2011 David and I were married in San Francisco and we gave many readings together until shortly before he passed. In 2015, Pureland Audio released his second poetry CD, *Two-Tone Poetry & Jazz,* featuring the poetry of David and I, and the music of our friend, saxophonist Zan Stewart.

David Meltzer was born under a lucky star, as they say, and his astrological chart reflects this with a configuration known as a "Star of David", an ancient symbol with various mystical meanings. A treasured mentor for many and a friend to everyone, David died at home as I prayed by his side. He said his speechless good-byes to family and friends and was carried "onward" near dawn on New Year's Eve, 2016, just a few weeks shy of his 80th birthday. Many Tibetan Buddhist masters and practitioners blessed his send off. Six literary memorials honored him during the following year, the last hosted by City Lights Booksellers at San Francisco State University. He will always be deeply missed and loved. David held his own light for the world.

———————

Jerome Rothenberg, poet, translator and anthologist, said, "David Meltzer had set out, when he was very young, to write a long poem called *The History of Everything,* an ambition that his later poetry brought ever closer to fulfillment. Regarding his book, *Two-Way Mirror,* I know of no better amalgam of poetry & poetics & no better introduction to the ways in which poetry can emerge for us & lead us beyond ourselves & toward our own fulfillments. Meltzer's grace of mind & the life of poetry that surrounds it make the case complete."

Diane di Prima, former San Francisco Poet Laureate says of him, "David Meltzer is a hidden adept, one of the secret treasures on our planet. Great poet, musician, comic; mystic unsurpassed, performer with few peers."

Lawrence Ferlinghetti, Beat Poet, author, publisher and founder of City Lights, has described David Meltzer as "one of the greats of post-WWII San Francisco poets and musicians."

ACKNOWLEDGEMENTS

Neeli Cherkovski and Clark Coolidge were initial provocateurs of this project from the get go. Close pals of David's they have long numbered among his devoted readers. This book would not have happened without their enthusiastic nudging.

Marina Lazzara's included commentary enhances the opportunity for readers to dig deeper into the extensive terrain of David's life work. Deep thanks to Marina for being up for the 'extra' work when asked!

Nicholas James Whittington gave detailed feedback proving essential to some of the thornier editorial concerns.

Other folks whose support and love for David and his work gave lasting encouragement include Micah Ballard, Garrett Caples, Ava Koohbor, and Sunnylyn Thibodeaux.

& very special thanks to Julie Rogers, David's wife, for being supportive and positive all through this project, and for her considerable time spent gathering memories, photos, and varied ephemera— exemplifying the love and devotion she has for David and his work, and her urge to preserve and share it.

May *Rock Tao* keep us all and many a reader rockin' ever Onward.

Patrick James Dunagan lives in San Francisco and works at Gleeson Library for the University of San Francisco. A graduate of the Poetics program from the now-defunct New College of California he edited *Roots and Routes: Poetics at New College of California*, eds. Patrick James Dunagan, Marina Lazzara, Nicholas James Whittington (Vernon Press) an anthology of critical writings by Poetics program alumni and faculty. He also edited a Portfolio of work on and by David Meltzer for Dispatches from the Poetry Wars (where he served on the editorial board). In addition, he edited poet Owen Hill's *A Walk Among the Bogus* (Lavender Ink). His essays and book reviews appear frequently with a wide number of both online and print publications. His most recent books include: *"There are people who think that painters shouldn't talk": A Gustonbook* (Post Apollo), *Das Gedichtete* (Ugly Duckling), from *Book of Kings* (Bird and Beckett Books), *Drops of Rain / Drops of Wine* (Spuyten Duyvil), *The Duncan Era: One Reader's Cosmology* (Spuyten Duyvil), and *Sketch of the Artist* (fmsbw). *After the Banished* is forthcoming from Empty Bowl Press.

Marina Lazzara received an MA/MFA in Poetics from New College of California and has published in various literary magazines and with Two Way Mirror Books. She is a vocalist and guitarist for the San Francisco band, The Rabbles and teaches Creative Writing and Health Education with Community Living Campaign. With Patrick Dunagan and Nicholas Whittington, she edited *Roots & Routes: Poetics at New College of California*, Vernon, 2020. Forthcoming is a book of selected work called *The Public Sound*, from fmsbw Press.